PŪJĀ AND SAṂSKĀRA

Pūjā
and
Saṃskāra

MUSASHI TACHIKAWA
SHOUN HINO
LALITA DEODHAR

MOTILAL BANARSIDASS PUBLISHERS
PRIVATE LIMITED • DELHI

Reprint : Delhi, 2006

First Edition : Delhi, 2001

ISBN: 81-208-1751-6

MOTILAL BANARSIDASS
41 U.A. Bungalow Road, Jawahar Nagar, Delhi 110 007
8 Mahalaxmi Chamber, 22 Bhulabhai Desai Road, Mumbai 400 026
236, 9th Main III Block, Jayanagar, Bangalore 560 011
203 Royapettah High Road, Mylapore, Chennai 600 004
Sanas Plaza, 1302 Baji Rao Road, Pune 411 002
8 Camac Street, Kolkata 700 017
Ashok Rajpath, Patna 800 004
Chowk, Varanasi 221 001

Printed in India
BY JAINENDRA PRAKASH JAIN AT SHRI JAINENDRA PRESS,
A-45 NARAINA, PHASE-I, NEW DELHI 110 028
AND PUBLISHED BY NARENDRA PRAKASH JAIN FOR
MOTILAL BANARSIDASS PUBLISHERS PRIVATE LIMITED,
BUNGALOW ROAD, DELHI 110 007

Preface

This book treats two representative Hindu rituals of contemporary India, Pūjā (offering service) and Saṃskāra (initiation rituals at important occasions of life). Saṃskāra rites are performed at significant junctures of an individual's life, from birth to death, by the individual's family. Pūjā rites, rather than being performed in relation to the life cycle of an individual in a family, are more deeply related to the annual rituals of the cult to which an individual or the person's family belongs. Persons may go to a temple and request priests to perform Pūjā rites, or they may perform them themselves at home.

For people living in India, Pūjā and Saṃskāra are not at all uncommon. Pūjā rites are performed everywhere—at temples, in private homes, on street corners—and although in recent times families observing all the traditional Saṃskāra rites have declined in number, almost all Hindu families still perform the major Saṃskāra. It is difficult, however, for those living outside India to know how these rites are performed. Hence, this book presents a large number of photographs that enable readers to gain an accurate grasp of them.

I define religion as a form of purposive action performed with consciousness of the distinction between the sacred and the profane. Religious activity may be broadly divided, according to the goal aimed at, into two kinds: (1) that which takes as its goal the spiritual well-being of the individual; and (2) that which has the purpose of enabling the group or the society to operate smoothly (festivals, initiation rites, etc.).

The Saṃskāra rites treated in this book belong to the category of group religious activities. Pūjā rites also originally belonged to this category, but in later times came to possess the aspect of individual religious cultivation for the purpose of the person's spiritual well-being.

Individual religious activity is frequently performed by individuals, but it is not limited to activities performed alone. Group religious activity is supported by the group, but it is common for individual religious activity to be included. An example is the case in which the acts performed by saints for their own spiritual salvation become the kernel for a festival held as the group religious activity of those gathered around such saints.

Individual and group religious activities are relatively clearly split in Buddhism and Hinduism. Religious activity centered on individual activity for departing from transmigration in the world of ignorance and aiming at the attainment of spiritual beatitude (emancipation, *nirvāṇa*) is accomplished by those who have renounced house-holding life. Originally, Buddhism was for such a group, and acts for extinguishing afflicting passions and attaining *nirvāṇa* were only possible for monks who had abandoned family and the social life of the locality. Hinduism provided different laws (*dharma*) for those who had families and maintained positions within the society and nation, as opposed to those who renounced house-holding life. Marriage, criminal and commercial law were not necessary for those who renounced worldly life and endeavoured in individual religious activity. Especially in India, distinction was made between those who sought emancipation from the world of transmigration and those who sought such this-worldly benefits as honor, power, and wealth. It is possible to label these two kinds of action world-negating and world-affirming. In India, they were called quiescence (*nivṛtti*) and advance (*pravṛtti*). Yoga practitioners and monks chose the former way of life, warriors and merchants the latter.

With regard to individual religious action, the sacred indicates that which is lofty and pure: Buddha, god, enlightenment, salvation, and so on. With regard to group religious activity, it indicates the dead, angry spirits, holy days, sacred sites, and so on. On the other hand, the profane, in terms of individual religious activity, is that which is to be negated through religious cultivation: unenlightened human existence, ignorance, afflicting passions, and so on. In terms of group religious activity, it is the everyday: the living, ordinary days, ordinary houses, and so on. Thus, the meaning of the sacred and the profane differs depending on the category of religious activity.

The difference between individual religious activity and group religious activity may be illustrated as follows.

In illustration [I], there are three configurations of rectangles. The rectangle placed above represents the realm of the sacred, the two below, the realm of the profane. When the profane begins to move toward the sacred, the sacred has yet to manifest itself to the profane in a way apprehensible to it, and there is only a medium possessing the direction from the profane to the sacred [I a]. At the moment there is a manifestation of the sacred, there appears a medium possessing the direction from the sacred to the profane [I b]. After there has been a manifestation of the sacred, then just as before, there exists a medium possessing the direction from the profane to the sacred, and at the same time, there is also a medium from the sacred to the profane. Hence, as seen in [I c], from the moment after reaching stage b, two vectors possessing different directions are present.

In [I a] and [I c], the upward arrow is slanted; this indicates that the medium includes temporal succession. In [I b] and [I c], the downward arrow is vertical; this expresses the temporal immediacy of the medium. However, in Buddhism, particularly Mahāyāna Buddhism, it is more accurate for the rectangles indicating the sacred and the profane to overlap, as in illustration [II], to express the sacred imminent in the profane.

On the other hand, in religions in which group rites are the medium (group religions), the profane, which is a state without tension or impurity, needs no rites for purification. These are ordinary conditions when there are no occasions of tension such as death, birth, and marriage (illustration [III a]). However, once an event such as a relative's death occurs, the ordinary condition of the profane changes and a condition of the sacred harboring tension arises. This condition of the sacred has become impure through death. In this case, in the sacred itself there is the impure. It is the sacred because it has the power to give rise to awe (illustration [III b]). Concerning funeral rites, each relative's individual, subjective religious practice is performed separately, and when a number of days have passed after death, the impure condition arising because of death is purified through the power of the rites [III b']. Here, the direction in the vector from the impure to the pure becomes unnecessary and disappears. The vector that has ceased to possess direction becomes a directionless quantity; in terms of religious cultivation, it is powerless and must vanish. Hence, the medium that has lost the direction from the impure to the pure cannot sustain itself further. In this way, in place of a sacred that had harbored a tension between the impure and the pure, the ordinary profane is born a second time [III a']. This condition continues until another event of some kind occurs or until a specified day. In this form of religious activity, even though persons may actively participate in a rite, they participate according to the customs of the group to which they belong, and their own

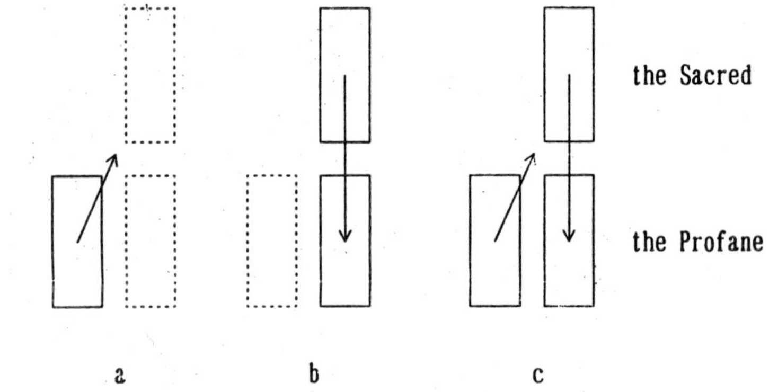

I. The Sacred and the Profane in individual religious activity

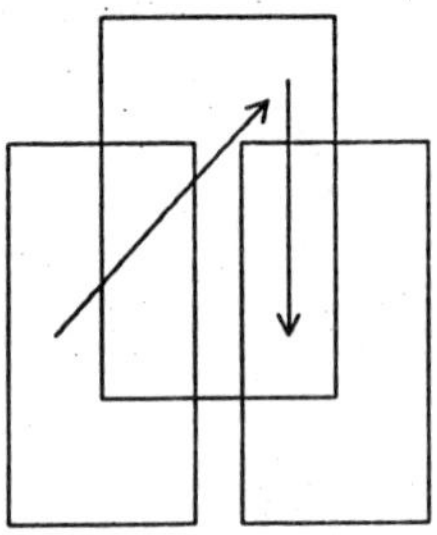

II. The Unity of the Sacred and the Profane

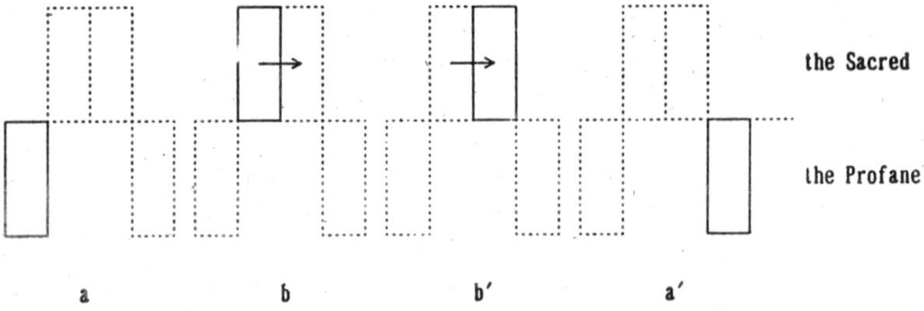

III. The Sacred and the Profane in group religious activity

daily life (the individual's realm of the profane) is not reflected on or negated. Here, the movement from the profane to the sacred does not occur through the negation of the subjective self, but arises through an outside event in which sacred time, place, and event are specified. In such a case, the vector is directed only within the sacred (for example, from the impure to another direction of the sacred, that is, the pure) and not from the profane to the sacred.

These two forms of religious activity—individual and group—are the original forms of the structure of religion, and almost all religions possess them together as two aspects. How these two forms coexist differs according to the specific religion. An example of religion in which the two are held in balance is Tantrism, including both Buddhist and Hindu versions. In Tantrism, the first form—individual subjective cultivation—takes the form of group religious activity and becomes ritualized, and at the same time, from this second form of religion—ancient initiation ceremonies, sexual rites, blood and bone rites, Shamanism, etc.—individual elements are absorbed into the organized doctrinal system and regarded as internalized rites (Eliade). For example, individual cultivation in Yoga practice may be placed among group rites without losing its original subjective, individual meaning, and ancient group religious survivals like blood rites come to hold new and different symbolic meanings and functions in the theoretical system of Tantrism. This book is intended not merely to introduce Pūjā and Saṃskāra rituals, but to indicate the place of ritual in the total structure of religion.

Part I is a revised version of Tachikawa's paper entitled "A Hindu Worship Service in Sixteen Steps, *Shoḍaśa-upacāra-pūjā*," *Bulletin of the National Museum of Ethnology*, Vol. 8 no. 1, March 1983, pp. 104-186.

Contents

PART II

A SIXTEEN SAṂSKĀRAS HANDED DOWN BY THE HIRAṆYAKEŚINS

PART I

A Hindu Worship Service in Sixteen Steps, Ṣoḍaśa-upacāra-pūjā

Introduction

One of the most popular Hindu rituals to felicitate the sacred is called *Ṣoḍaśa-upacāra-pūjā* (Worship Service in Sixteen Steps). This paper illustrates the *Ṣoḍaśa-upacāra-pūjā* performed in Catuḥśṛṅgī Temple, Poona, Maharashtra, India, on the morning of the twenty-seventh of August, 1981.

Every religion is characterized by the distinction between the sacred and the profane. These two poles are not isolated points at the edges of the universe, since a dynamic relationship exists between them. The profane violates the territory of the sacred, while the latter wants to distinguish itself from the former. As long as the power or function of the profane remains, the sacred has difficulty in appearing in the world. That is, in order for the sacred to manifest itself, the profane has to be destroyed. The two religious poles are thus found in such an unsympathetic relationship that each denies the existence of the other. We know, however, that the profane makes desparate efforts to approach the sacred. It is through the power of rituals or practices that the dynamic relationship between the two poles becomes possible. Ritual is a form of human action in which the profane is trying to obtain the power of the sacred.

One of the commonest forms of such human actions found in India is *pūjā* (worship, offering). The term "*pūjā*" derives from the root *pūj*, to make offering.[1] That which is offered is one of the indispensable elements of *pūjā*. The materials to be offered in *pūjā* are various. A great number of animals such as buffalos and goats are offered even today, and it was reported that human flesh was offered in some parts of India, as happened elsewhere. Nowadays, however, in most Indian temples, water, fruits, flowers, and the like are offered. What is offered in *pūjās* is not necessarily corporeal or tangible, for devotees often offer their minds to the gods.

Offering is made not only in *pūjā* but also in other types of religious actions. For example, in *homa* sacrifice, which should be distinguished from *pūjā*, materials such as ghee and rice-cakes are offered to fire. Offering, which comprises the world of the profane, is the most basic means adopted by humans to enter into a rela-

1. For its etymological meaning, see [Charpentier 1927: 93], [Thieme 1939: 105].

tionship with the sacred. Let us note here that offerings are determined to be destroyed or "killed." In Kathmandu, a huge number of buffalos and goats are slain on the days of the Durgā *pūjā*. The ghee (clarified butter) and rice-cakes offered in *homa* sacrifice are consumed by fire. When water, fruits, flowers, and the like have been offered in *pūjā,* they no longer belong to the world of the profane. When those things such as flowers and fruits are offered to the sacred or to its image, their religious value is changed. That offerings are destined to be destroyed implies that the profane must "die" to obtain "rebirth."

Offerings such as animals are substitutions for humans who act as the sacrificers. By killing animals on the altar, humans experience a symbolic death, since the animals "die" in place of humans. By giving part of their property to others, those who perform rituals show to the sacred that they are lessening their power, even if they are not actually sacrificing their lives.

Another basic aspect of *pūjā* is that it must possess that to which offering is made.[2] Offering is always made to someone or to something. The blood of scapegoats is offered to the terrifying Goddess Durgā. In the *Ṣoḍaśa-upacāra-pūjā* (Worship Service in Sixteen Steps), materials such as water, flower, and garments are generally offered to deities. Usually it is to a divinity that offering is made. We need not discuss here whether the offering is made to the image of a divinity or to that which is symbolized by the image. In our system, however, it would be safe to designate 'that to which the offering is made' as the sacred. That to which the offering is made does not necessarily have a concrete image. A *pūjā* can be performed even to a particular kind of atmosphere, if the atmosphere is believed to have sacred power.

Having bought offering materials such as flowers and fruits at the gate of a temple, people come to the main hall, and ask the priests to perform *pūjās*. In temples, *pūjās* are usually performed by priests. Those who perform *pūjās,* however, need not be priests, for the head of each Hindu family is supposed to worship gods daily. A patron and his wife participated in performing the worship in sixteen steps in Nāgeśvar Temple (see Appendix I).

2. cf. [Hubert & Mauss 1964: 10], [Malamond 1976: 15].

The procedure of *Ṣoḍaśa-upacāra-pūjā* may be divided into two parts: preliminaries (A) and main worship (B).[3] (For the signs: A and B, see Contents.) The preparation for the *pūjā* is done in the former. First the priest purifies himself by sipping water (*ācamana*) (A–1). Then he controls his breath (A–2). Next he recites the Gāyatrīmantra (A–3) and contemplates the divinities (A–4). By these four actions the priest becomes ready to perform the worship service. Then he declares the performance and the purpose of the *pūjā* (A–5). Next, in order to get rid of obstacles for the *pūjā*, the priest worships God Gaṇapati (A–6). This deity is often worshipped before something is undertaken. Now that the priest himself has become ready to perform the *pūjā*, he is going to consecrate the ritual utensils, such as the pot, the conch, the bell, and the lamp (A–7, 8). At the last stage of the "preliminaries" (A), the priest consecrates himself and the materials for worship by sprinkling water (A–9).

The main worship (B) consists of sixteen steps, the first five of which are:

1. Invocation to the deity (*āvāhana*)
2. Offering the seat (*āsana*)
3. Offering water for washing the feet of the deity (*pādya*)
4. Offering sacred water (*arghya*)
5. Offering water for rinsing the mouth (*ācamanīya*)

Here the priest treats the deity just as one treats a guest. Yet human guests visit the houses of their friends; the deities have to be invoked to visit the houses of human beings. Similarly, when a guest has arrived, he is offered a seat, water for washing his feet, and the like.

The sixth step, i.e., bathing (*snāna*), which is the most important part of the Worship Service in Sixteen Steps, may be portioned into three:

6–(1)~(5) Bathing the deity with the five ambrosia (*pañcāmṛta*), i.e., milk (*payas*), curds (*dadhi*), ghee (*ghṛta*, clarified butter), honey (*madhu*), and sugar (*śarkara*).

6–(6)~(8) The priest bathes the deity with fragrant water (*gandhodaka*) and anoints it with yellow powder

3. cf. [Aiyangar 1940: 4, 35], [Kane 1974: 726ff.], [Citrav 1977: 24], [Heiler 1959: 378], [Joshi n.d.], [Manjul 1967: 29], [Matsubara 1967], [Renou & Filliozа 1947: 573], [Tachikawa 1981: 71].

(*haridrā*) and red powder (*kuṃkuma*) on the divine image. Then he offers flowers and a lamp to the deity.

6–(9) The last part is consecration (*abhiṣeka*) with water.

In the *Ṣoḍaśa-upacāra-pūjā* performed in Catuḥśṛṅgī Temple, the consecration (*abhiṣeka*) with water was done with the recitations of some Vedic passages: *Puruṣasūkta* (*Ṛgveda,* X, 90, 1–16), *Śrīsūkta* (*Ṛgveda,* V, 87), *Rudra* (*Kṛṣṇa Yajurveda,* IV, 5, 1–11), and *Vasor dhārā* (*Kṛṣṇa Yajurveda,* IV, 7, 1–11). In the *Ṣoḍaśa-upacāra-pūjā* performed in Nāgeśvar Temple, Poona (cf. Appendix I), among the above-mentioned four Vedic passages only *Puruṣasūkta* was recited, and some Vedic hymns belonging to Viṣṇu were recited. The Vedic passages to be recited at this stage differ according to the identity of the main deity to be worshipped.

The next seven steps (B-7~13) may be considered as comprising one group:

7. Offering the garment (*vastra*)
8. Offering the upper garment (*upavastra*)
9. Offering fragrant materials (*gandha*)
10. Offering flowers (*puṣpa*)
11. Offering incense (*dhūpa*)
12. Offering the lamp (*dīpa*) and fragrant materials (*gandha*)
13. Offering food (*naivedya*)

The guest who has taken a bath is now offered the garment, the upper garment, fragrant materials, flowers incense, and food. After the food (*naivedya*) has been given, a *tāmbūla* (a leaf of betel together with areca-nuts, catechu, and spices)[4] is often offered, as seen in the *pūjā* performed in Nāgeśvar Temple (cf. Fig. 104).

The next step is especially endowed with a religious value:

14. Going around the divine image clockwise (*pradakṣiṇā*)

The priest goes around the image of the deity clockwise so that the right side of the priest is always turned toward the image of the sacred. This is a way of making a reverential salutation to someone.[5] At this stage the deity has been fully adorned with garments, flowers, and fragrant materials. Now that the sacred has manifested its full form before the eyes of the priests or devotees, the priest or the patron of the *pūjā* will felicitate the theophany by

4. [Apte 1978: 768].
5. [Apte 1978: 1091].

walking around the image clockwise or by waving the lamp. This is the climax of the *Ṣoḍaśa-upacāra-pūjā*.

Since the deity has been treated properly (*satkṛta*), he who feels satisfied (*prasanna*) is going back. It is in the last two steps that the priest or the patron makes salutation to the deity and send him or her off.

15. Salutation (*namaskāra*).
16. Offering flowers with the recitation of mantra (*mantrapuṣpa*).

The last step is also called *visarjana,* i.e., sending forth, or allowing the deity invoked to return.

Pūjās are always performed with some purpose. Most of the people coming to Catuḥśṛṅgī Temple seem to request the performance of *pūjās* in order to obtain secular success such as wealth, health, or the birth of a son. They do not completely believe that those rituals have real magical power which would enable them to obtain whatever they want. Nonetheless, they come to temples and "obtain the *prasāda* so that they can feel refreshed and encouraged." Some, however, do not come for secular purposes, since there are those who come to temples such as Catuḥśṛṅgī Temple to seek ultimate spiritual enlightenment.

There remains to be mentioned one of the most remarkable things about *Ṣoḍaśa-upacāra-pūjā,* the worship service (*pūjā*) consisting of sixteen ways of showing reverence (*upacāra*). That is to say, each *upacāra* begins with the recitation of each verse of the *Puruṣasūkta* (*Ṛgveda,* X, 90), which consists of sixteen verses. Accordingly, the first *upacāra,* i.e., the invocation (*āvāhana*) to the deity, starts with the recitation of the first verse of the *Puruṣasūkta.* The second *upacāra* begins with that of the second verse, and so on. It is obvious, however, that the content of the *Puruṣasūkta* does not correspond to the procedure of the service, although it deals with the offering of the primordial man (*puruṣa*).

The *Puruṣasūkta* belonging to the *Taittirīyāraṇyaka* of the *Black Yajurveda,* however, consists of eighteen verses. Accordingly, the worship of the schools keeping that type of *Puruṣasūkta* has eighteen steps. For example, those Brahmans belonging to the Hiraṇyakeśī Branch observe the worship service consisting of the eighteen steps, which are enumerated in List 1. The fifteenth verse of the 16 verses edition missing in the 18 verses edition of *Puruṣasūkta.*[6] The sixteenth and the seventeenth verses of the 18

6. For the text of the 18 verses edition of the *Puruṣasūkta,* see [Limaye & Bhide 1981].

verses edition are missing in the other edition. This, however, makes little difference in the procedure of the *Ṣoḍaśa-upacāra-pūjā*.

Another important aspect of *Ṣoḍaśa-upacāra-pūjā* is that it is the norm or frame of Hindu god worship. Various kinds of deities are worshipped in this frame with slight modifications. Although the main purpose of this book is to illustrate the general procedure of the *Ṣoḍaśa-upacāra-pūjā* performed at Catuḥśṛṅgī Temple, Poona, it includes general surveys of two other *Ṣoḍaśa-upacāra-pūjās* in Appendices I and II. The main deity of the worship at Catuḥśṛṅgī Temple is Goddess Catuḥśṛṅgī, who is believed to be an incarnation of the wife of God Śiva. This male god is one of the three main Hindu deities. The other two are Viṣṇu and Brahman. The main deities of the second *Ṣoḍaśa-upacāra-pūjā* treated in Appendix I are Vittal and his wife Rukmiṇī. The former, an incarnation of Viṣṇu, is popular especially in the state of Maharashtra. The main deity

List 1

16 steps	18 steps	the name of the step	Skt.	the number used in this book
1	1	contemplation	*dhyāna*	A–4
2	2	offering the seat	*āsana*	B–2
3	3	offering the water for washing the feet	*pādya*	B–3
4	4	offering the sacred water	*arghya*	B–4
5	5	offering the water for washing the mouth	*ācamanīya*	B–5
6	6	offering a mixture of honey	*madhuparka*	B–6
	7	bathing	*snāna*	
7	8	offering the garment	*vastra*	B–7
8	9	offering the sacred thread	*yajñopavīta*	B–8
9	10	offering fragrant materials	*gandha*	B–9
10	11	offering flowers	*puṣpa*	B–10
11	12	offering incense	*dhūpa*	B–11
12	13	offering the lamp	*dīpa*	B–12
13	14	offering food	*naivedya*	B–13
14	15	offering betel leaf	*tāmbūla*	
	16	offering presents	*daksiṇā*	B–14
	17	offering fruits		
16	18	offering flowers with salutation	*puṣpāñjali*	B–16

of the third *Ṣoḍaśa-upacāra-pūjā* treated in Appendix II is Gaṇapati, "Chief of the Gaṇas" (demigod attendants on Śiva). He is depicted as having an elephant's head with one broken tusk and a fat paunch. Although he is said to be the second son of Śiva and his wife Pārvatī, he is revered not only by Śaivites (those who worship Śiva) but also by Vaiṣṇavites (those who worship Viṣṇu). The main deities of those three worships thus differ from one another. Their procedures are, however, almost the same.

It was at my request that the worship service was performed at Catuḥśṛṅgī Temple on the twenty-seventh of August, 1981. A week before its performance, I paid eleven rupees (about one dollar and a half) at the counter of the main hall of the temple. Having filled out a form, a priest gave it to me as the receipt. When a week later four of us reached the temple, two priests were making preparations for the *pūjā* in its sanctuary, where the *pūja* was going to be performed. It began at 8 : 18 A. M., and ended at 9 : 48 A. M. While it was being performed, I was engaged in photographing it. Mr. Suenaga, who accompanied me, was taking 8 mm movie films. Mr. Asai was noting the number and time of each of my photographs. Miss Kate was not only recording the recitations of the ritual text but also pointing out for me each step of the worship.

It is not determined when a *Ṣoḍaśa-upacāra-pūjā* should be performed. It may be performed any day if a patron (*yajamāna*) makes a request to the priest in a temple. The place for its performance is not confined to a temple. As a matter of fact, the householder of a Brahman family is recommended to perform this worship in his house. The *Ṣoḍaśa-upacāra-pūjā* may be performed either in the morning or in the evening, as we shall see later. During even my short stays in Poona (one month of 1975, three months of 1977, ten days of 1979, one month of 1981, and one week of 1982), I found it quite easy to have numerous opportunities to see *Ṣoḍaśa-upacāra-pūjās* being performed. In Poona City, I was able to observe simple *pūjās,* if not the elaborate *pūjā* in sixteen steps, being performed daily in almost every Hindu house. *Pūjās* are thus alive in the Poona area. I requested the priests at Catuḥśrṅgī Temple to perform the worship in the same manner as they would at the request of Hindu devotees. As far as I could see, the worship service at Catuḥśṛṅgī Temple was performed in the ordinary manner. Hence, I believe that the worship service performed at Catuḥśṛṅgī Temple in August of 1981 may be considered as exemplary of the *Ṣoḍaśa-upacāra-pūjās* that are nowadays performed in the Poona area.

Except for Nos. 95, 97, 99, and 108–125, which were taken by Mr. H. Hori, all photographs used here were taken by the author. Those used in Temple of Goddess Catuḥśṛṅgī (pp. 13~28) were taken on August 18, 1981, except No. 1 (Aug. '77). Those in Worship Service in Catuḥśṛṅgī Temple (pp. 30~63) were taken on August 27, 1981; and those in Appendix I, on August 22, 1981; and those in Appendix II, on January 14, 1982. Those in Note 35 were taken on August 25, 1979. A Nikon camera (Photomic A, f=50 mm/ 1 : 1.2) was used to take the photographs related to Catuḥśṛṅgī Temple (pp. 10~61) except for those in Note 35, which were taken with a Konica C35 (f=38 mm/1 : 2.8). For those in Appendix I, I used a Konica C35 and Mr. Hori used an Olympus XA2 (f=35 mm/1 : 3.5). For those in Appendix II, a Pentax MVI (f=28 mm/ 1: 2.8) was used. Except for those in the section on Catuḥśṛṅgī Temple a stroboscopic lamp was always used. The illustrations used in Part I have been drawn by tracing photographs printed from 35 mm negative films, which had been made from 8 mm movie films, as the photographs made from 8 mm movie films did not come out clearly. I wish to express my deepest gratitude to Prof. V. N. Jha (Center of Advanced Studies in Sanskrit, Poona University), who answered my questions about the *Ṣoḍaśa-upacāra-pūjā*, when he was staying in Nagoya, during the fall of 1981. I would also like to thank Miss A. Kate (Research Fellow, Poona University in 1981) who helped me to photograph the service performed in Catuḥśṛṅgī Temple in August of 1981.

I owe a special debt of gratitude to the priests of Catuḥśṛṅgī Temple who permitted me to photograph their service. Prof. S. Bahulkar (Sanskrit College, Tilak Maharashtra Vidyapeeth, Poona) was of great help to me in observing the Great Worship (*mahāpūjā*), an elaborate form of *Ṣoḍaśa-upacāra-pūjā*, performed in the same temple in the summer of 1979. I must also thank Mr. H. Hori, Mr. A. Suenaga, and Mr. N. Asai, from whom I received assistance during research in Poona in the summer of 1981. Thanks also should go to Miss Yūko Yagami, who typed this manuscript and drew illustrations by tracing the photographs. Finally, I would like to express my deepest gratitude to Mrs. Christine Ogawa who rendered a great service in improving my English.

Temple of Goddess Catuḥśṛṅgī

Entrance to the Temple

Catuḥśṛṅgī temple is situated on the side of a small hill in the western part of Poona, India.[7] The main deity worshiped is Goddess Catuḥśṛṅgī, or 'Goddess with four horns.' Probably "horn" means the peak of a hill or a mountain. Goddess Catuḥśṛṅgī is said to be an incarnated form of the Goddess Saptaśṛṅgī ('Goddess with seven horns') who is believed to reside in a mountain in Nasik, 220 km north of Poona. The name of "Saptaśṛiṅgī" is on the list of the one hundred and eight holy places (*śāktapīṭha*) included in the *Devībhāgavata*.[8] According to the tradition of Catuḥśṛṅgī Temple, Goddess Saptaśṛiṅgī in Nasik manifested herself at the very location of the present Catuḥśṛiṅgī Temple to a devotee who had become unable to visit Nasik on account of old age. A naturally carved rock formation found on the slope of the hill is regarded as an image of Goddess Catuḥśṛṅgī.

For several decades the Angal family, who belongs to Deśastha Brahman, has been in charge of this temple. A few priests belonging to the Angal family are sent to take care of the temple for one or two years. In the summer of 1981, the priests of the temple began to renovate the temple. When I visited it in September of 1982, renovation had been completed.

The Angal family has employed a young Deśastha Brahman, Mr. Kulkarni, to stay in the temple and perform daily services. As we shall see later, two priests performed the worship in sixteen steps, of which records have been taken in this book. The performing priest who sits in front of the divine image is a son of the Angal family (see Fig. 34); the prompting priest, who assists the performing priest, is Mr. Kulkarṇi. They said that they performed a simple form of worship, in sixteen steps, early every morning.

7. cf. Appendix III.
8. *Devībhāgavata*, 7, 38, 6; cf. [Sircar 1973: 107].

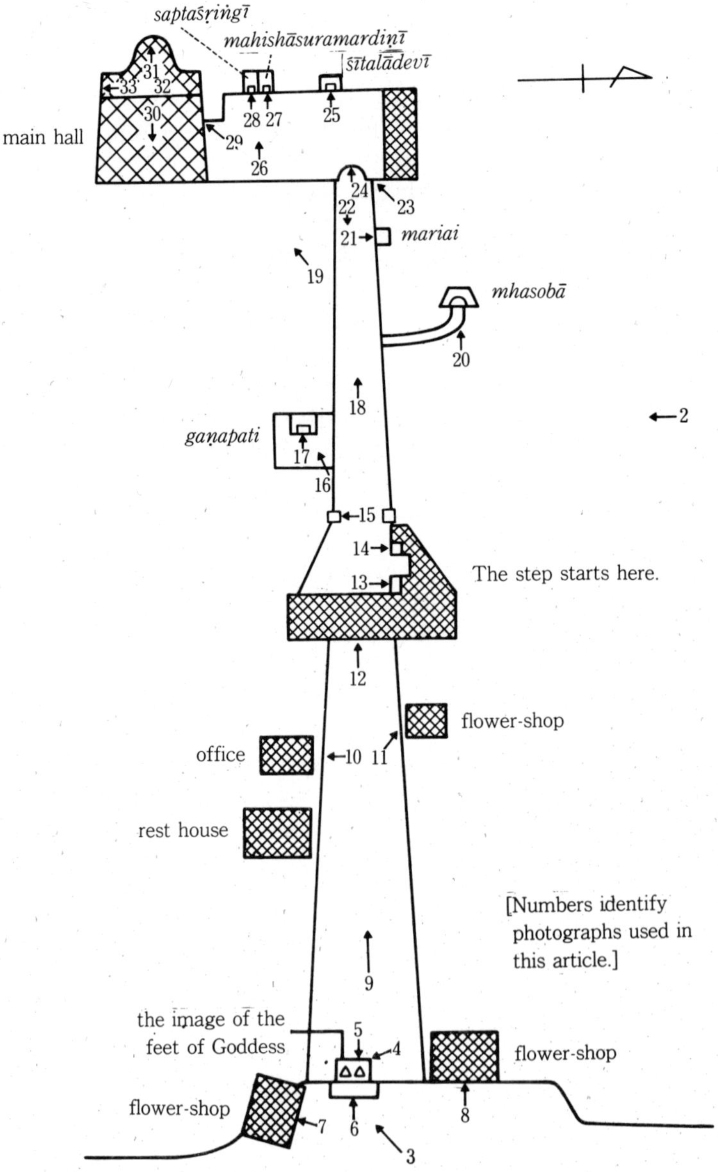

Fig. 1 An Illustration of Catuḥśṛṅgī Temple.

Fig. 2 The temple of Goddess Catuḥśṛṅgī is situated on the side of a hill.

Fig. 3 People are gathering at the gate of the temple. Each deity has its favourite day of the week. Tuesday is the day for goddesses. (The photographs Figs. 2–33 were taken on August 18 Tuesday 1981.)

Fig. 4 Detail of Fig. 3. The image of the feet of Goddess Catuḥśṛṅgī is covered with flowers.

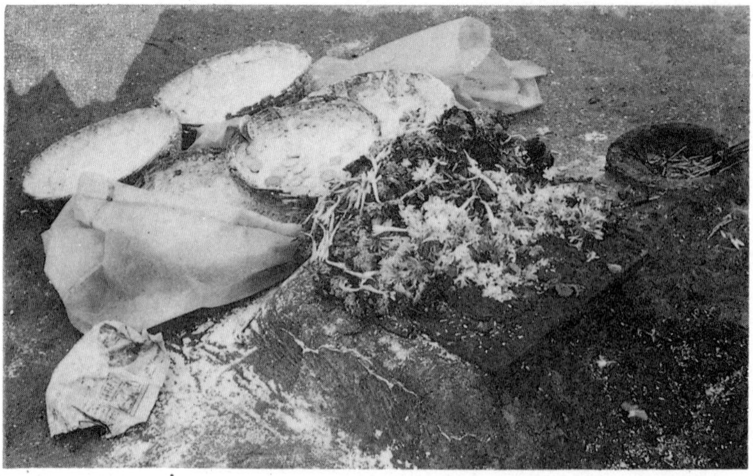

Fig. 5 Detail of Fig. 4. When these flowers are removed, the image of the Goddess' feet can be seen (see Fig. 6).

Fig. 6 Those who have no time to go to the main hall of the temple do homage to this image of the feet of Goddess Catuḥśṛṅgī.

Fig. 7 This woman has been selling coconuts, flowers, etc., at the gate of this temple for several years.

Fig. 8 A small cloth (Marth., *khaṇ*) is offered to the Goddess as her skirt. It must be green, the color of Nimba tree (*Azadirachta indica*).

Fig. 9 The road leads to the main hall of Catuḥśṛṅgī Temple. The main hall is visible on the side of the hill. The rest house and the temple office are on the left side of the road.

Fig. 10 At the temple office rituals can be requested. A number of rituals and their prices are listed on the right door of the office.

Fig. 11 There is a flower shop on the right side of the road leading to the main hall.

Images of Deities Associated with Goddess Catuḥśṛṅgī

Within Catuḥśṛṅgī Temple and its grounds, there are several shrines of deities associated with Goddess Catuḥśṛṅgī, such as Mhasobā, Mariai, Śītalā, Mahiṣāsuramardinī, Saptaśṛṅgī, and Gaṇapati.[9]

No. 13 Stone symbols of goddesses and Māruti
No. 14 *liṅgayoni*
No. 16 Shine of Gaṇapati
No. 20 Shrine of Demon Mhasobā
No. 21 Shrine of Goddess Mariai
Each number identifies the photo number in Fig. 1.

Fig. 12

Fig. 13 A boy worshipping goddesses (left) and Māruti (right), whose stone images are smeared with red powder. Māruti is another name of Hanumān. The cult of this god is prevalent in Maharashtra.

9. For Mhasobā, an aboriginal god especially popular in Maharashtra, see [Kosambi 1962: 181] and [Tachikawa 1981: 72]. For Mariai, goddesses of Southern origin, see [Tachikawa 1981: 72–73] and [Joshi 1972: 86–87]. There are a number of shrines of the goddess of Smallpox in Poona city, as in other Indian cities. These shrines are usually found under Pippala trees (*Ficus religiosa*). For the Gaṇapati cult in Poona, see [Hino 1981], [Hino 1982], and [Ikeda 1979].

Fig. 14 Symbol of *liṅga* and *yoni* (left). *Liṅga* is the phallic emblem of God Śiva, and functions as a symbol of the male creative principle. *Yoni* or the female generative organ is a symbol of the female creative energy. The *liṅga* standing on the *yoni* represents the union of the male and female principles. On the right side of the symbol of *liṅga* and *yoni*, stone images of local goddesses are seen.

Fig. 15 Symbol of *yoni*.

Fig. 16 People at the entrance of the Gaṇapati shrine. Most of those who come to Catuḥśṛṅgī Temple are ladies.

Fig. 17 The image of Gaṇapati in this shrine façes east, which means that this image is believed to bestow wealth. If Gaṇapati faces north, he bestows knowledge and ultimate beatitude.

Fig. 18 Steps leading to the main hall.

Fig. 19 The main hall of Catuḥśṛṅgī Temple.

Fig. 20 This is an image of Mhasobā, the most famous water-buffalo demon. He is said to have been killed by Goddess Mahiṣāsuramardiṇī. In Maharashtra State Mhasobā is particularly worshipped by farmers.

Fig. 21 Red painted stones represent Mariai Goddesses.

Fig. 22 A view from Mariai shrine.

Fig. 23 These are three stone goddesses which have been painted red.

Fig. 24 The first entrance to the main hall.

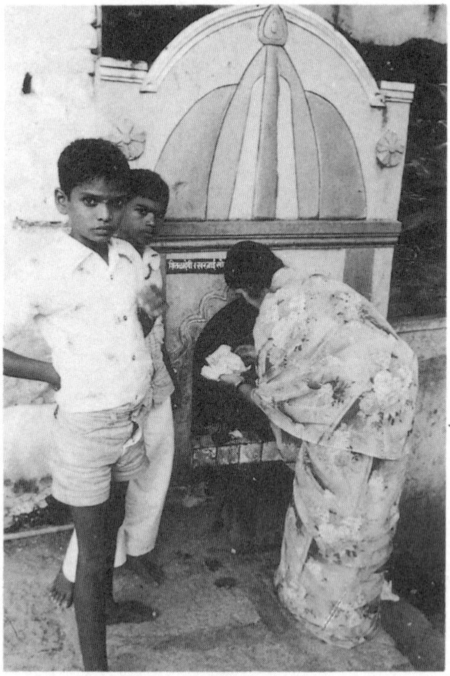

Fig. 25 When one passes through the first entrance to the main hall, one can find a small shrine of the goddess of Smallpox (Skt., *śītalādevī;* Marth., *sitalādevī*). This photograph shows a woman making an offering to the goddess, whose cult prevails in Poona as in other areas of India. The stone images of this goddess are similar to those of Mariai Goddesses.

Fig. 26 Images of Mahiṣāsuramardiṇī (right) and Saptaśṛṅgī (left).

Fig. 27 Mahiṣāsuramardiṇī (detail of Fig. 26).

Fig. 28 Saptaśṛṅgī (detail of Fig. 26). This image was replaced by a new statue of Goddess Saptaśṛṅgī in 1982.

Fig. 29 Entrances to the main hall. The image of Goddess Catuḥśṛṅgī is found at the bottom of the tower.

Main Hall of Catuḥśṛṅgī Temple

Fig. 30 A *homa*-altar is in the center of the western half of the main hall. (This photo was taken from the top of the steps leading to the sanctuary of the temple. cf. Fig. 32)

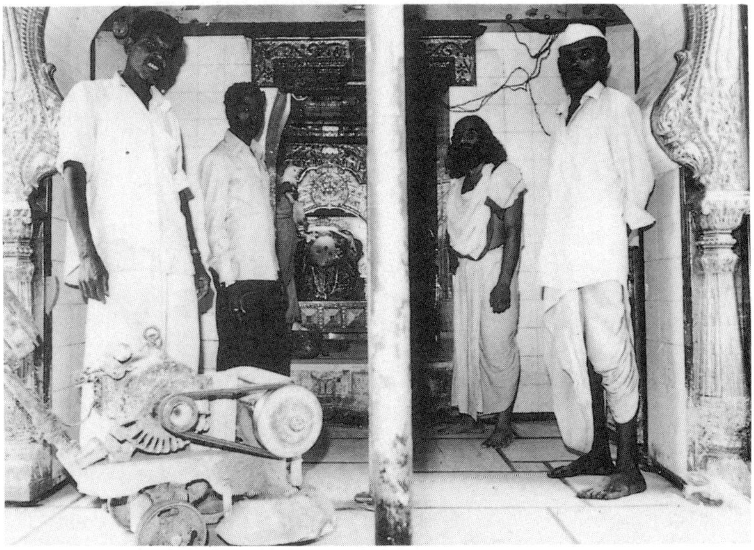

Fig. 31 Renovating the main hall. This photo shows the eastern half of the main hall. In the center of the photo one can see the sanctuary, where the *Ṣoḍaśa-upacāra-pūjā* is to be performed.

Fig. 32 (1) Relief of Bhairava and his wife. cf. Fig. 33. (2) Image of Goddess Catuḥśṛṅgī. cf. Fig. 83. (3) A stone image representing a minor goddess.

Fig. 33 On the left side of the sanctuary (cf. Fig. 32 (1)) there is a relief of Bhairava, the terrifying form of Śiva, and his consort. The erected *liṅga* is one of the main iconographic characteristics of Bhairava. A great number of aboriginal female divinities including Goddess Catuḥśṛṅgī were gradually identified with Śiva's wife.

A Worship Service in Sixteen Steps Performed at the Catuḥśṛṅgī Temple

(A) Preliminaries Performed by the Priest

(1) *Purification of self by Sipping Water* (*Ācamana*)

The worship begins with the following citation of the twenty-four epithets of God Viṣṇu.[10]

> "*keśavāya namaḥ, nārāyaṇāya namaḥ, mādhavāya namaḥ, govindāya namaḥ, viṣṇave namaḥ, madhusūdanāya namaḥ, trivikramāya namaḥ, vāmanāya namaḥ, śrīdharāya namaḥ, hṛṣīkeśāya namaḥ, padmanābhāya namaḥ, dāmodarāya namaḥ, saṅkarṣaṇāya namaḥ, vāsudevāya namaḥ, pradyumnāya namaḥ, puruṣottamāya namaḥ, adhokṣajāya namaḥ, nārasiṃhāya namaḥ, acyutāya namaḥ, janārdanāya namaḥ, upendrāya namaḥ, haraye namaḥ, śrīkṛṣṇāya namaḥ.*"[10]
>
> "Salutation to Keśava, Nārāyaṇa, Mādhava, Govinda, Viṣṇu, Madhusūdana, Trivikrama, Vāmana, Śrīdhara, Hṛṣīkeśa, Padmanābha, Damodara, Saṅkarṣaṇa, Vāsudeva, Pradyumna, Puruṣottama, Adhokṣaja, Nārasiṃha, Acyuta, Janārdana, Upendra, Hari, Śrīkṛṣṇa."

The worship is going to be performed mainly for Goddess Catuḥśṛṅgī, but it is general custom to recite the epithets of God Viṣṇu in the beginning of a *Ṣoḍaśa-upacāra-pūjā*. This seems to suggest that Worship Service in Sixteen Steps was originally formed in a Vaiṣṇava environment.

---

10. The priest recites the text of the entire service without the use of written materials. The text consists of ritual *mantras* and Vedic passages. The former indicates each step of the worship. In this book I will quote and translate important *mantras*. The latter of the text contains famous Vedic passages, such as *Puruṣasūkta* (*Ṛgveda*, X, 90) and *Śrīsūkta* (*Ṛgveda*, V, 87).
    I could not find any printed text or manuscript of this worship service. cf. [Joshi n.d. b]. This Joshi's book indicates that other services use almost the same text as the worship performed in the Catuḥśṛṅgī Temple; [Manjul 1967]. This book sheds useful light upon the process of the *Ṣoḍaśa-upacāra-pūjā*.

Fig. 34 Each time an epithet of Viṣṇu is mentioned in this step, the priest is supposed to sip water three times. In this service, however, he did not follow such a procedure. (The photographs Figs. 33-88 were taken on August 27, 1981.)

(2) *Control of Breathing* (*Prāṇāyāma*)

The priests recite the following formula for control of breathing: *oṃ bhūḥ oṃ bhuvaḥ oṃ svaḥ oṃ mahaḥ oṃ janaḥ oṃ tapaḥ oṃ satyam.*[11]

Fig. 35 The performing priest is lightly pressing his nostrils with his left hand. This is the way to control breathing.

11. Every Brahman is supposed to utter this formula at the commencement of his *sandhyā* (cf. Note 12). The syllable "*oṃ*" is uttered as a holy exclamation at the beginning of sacred syllables or words. The formula refers to the seven worlds starting with *bhūḥ* and ending with *satya* which is the abode of Brahman.

The worship is conducted by two priests: the performing priest and the prompting priest. Ritual actions are carried out by the former, and recitation is done by both. The worship is performed in the sanctuary (*garbhāghāra*) located in the western half of the main hall. The performing priest sits in front of the sacred image of Goddess Catuḥśṛṅgī, and the prompting priest recites formulae on the left side of the sanctuary.

(3) *Recitation of the Gāyatrīmantra*

The Gāyatrīmantra is recited:

"*oṃ tat savitur vareṇyaṃ bhargo devasya dhīmahi/ dhiyo yo naḥ pracodayāt//*"[12] (We meditate on that desirable light of the divine Savitṛ, who influences our pious rites.)[13]

Fig. 36 (1) stand, (2) the vessel for *kuṃkuma* (red powder) and *haridrā* (yellow powder) (cf. Fig. 67), (3) the small vessel for *kuṃkuma* and *haridrā* (Marth. *tripaḷe*), (4) water jar, (5) water pot, (6) lamp, (7) the pot of holy water (cf. Fig. 86), (8), (9) Small bowls (cf. Fig. 46), (10) flowers

"*Bhūḥ*," "*bhuvaḥ*," and "*svaḥ*" are the three mystic words (*vyāhṛti*). They mean, respectively, earth, ether, and heaven. *Mahaḥ* is the fourth of the seven worlds which extend one above the other from the earth. The fifth is *janaḥ*. [Apte 1978: 1247]. *Tapaḥ* is above *janaḥ*. *Satya* is the upper-most world. cf. [Citrav 1977b: 29], [Śendye 1981: 9].

12. This verse (*Ṛgveda*, III, 62, 10) is considered as sacred and is known as *Gāyatrīmantra*, which every Brahman is supposed to repeat at his *sandhyā* (morning and evening devotions) and other occasions. It is said that even great sins are expiated by a pious repetition of this verse [Apte 1978: 657]. cf. [Aufrecht 1968: Vol. 2, 271].

13. This is Wilson's translation [Wilson 1977: Vol. 3, 110]. For Gāyatrī hymns, see [Ḍev 1969: 8].

In order to purify himself, the priest performs the first three rites (A-1,2 and 3). According to the Hindu tradition, these rites are obligatory (*nitya*); that is, the 'twice-born' (*dvija*) are supposed to perform them everyday.

(4) *Contemplation of the Divinities* (*Dhyāna*)

In this step the priest contemplates "all divinities" (*sarvadevebhyaḥ*). Remembering their kindness and grace, the priest praises them. Although the worship by sixteen ways (*ṣodaśopacāra*) which is performed in this temple is offered to Goddess Catuḥśṛṅgī, the priest does homage to all divinities during this step.[14]

Fig. 37 The garment for Goddess Catuḥśṛṅgī can be seen in front of the prompting priest (cf. B-7).

(5) *Declaration of Performance and Purpose* (*Saṃkalpa*)

The priest declares that he will perform the *pūjā* "in order to

14. For the text of this step, see [Joshi n.d. b: 12-13].

please the supreme deity" (*parameśvaraprītyartham*).[15] Then, he mentions the exact time and place of the worship in astrological detail.

(6) *Worship of Gaṇapati* (*Gaṇapatipūjā*)

Ṛgveda (II, 23, 1) is recited:

> "We invoke three, Brahmaṇaspati, chief leader of the (heavenly) bands; a sage of sages; abounding beyond measure in [every kind of] food: best lord of prayer: hearing our invocations, come with thy protections, and sit down in the chamber of sacrifice."

The priest worships Gaṇapati by reciting this Vedic verse, which contains the term "Gaṇapati." It is, however, uncertain whether the term in this Vedic verse means the elephant-faced god. Gaṇapati is often worshipped when one begins to perform rituals or to write a book. For an image of Gaṇapati, see Fig. 17.

(7) *Consecration of the Pot, the Conch, and the Bell* (*Kalaśaśaṅkhaghaṇṭāpūjana*)

"*atha kalaśaśaṅkhaghaṇṭāpūjanam.*"

(Now [the time has come to] worship the pot, the conch, and the bell.)

Fig. 38 The priest is consecrating the pot by placing a flower on its rim.

15. When I visited Catuḥśṛṅgī Temple in the summer of 1982, Rev. Kurkarṇi recited the text as follows: "in order to please Mahākālī, Māhālakṣmī, and Mahāsarasvatī." cf. [Citrav 1977 b: 25].
16. cf. [Dandge 1977:9] This translation is quoted from [Wilson 1977: Vol. 2, 262-3].

Fig. 39 He is now filling the conch with water. Having done so, he pours water on the head of Goddess. Then he refills the conch and places it behind the pot.

"*ghaṇṭāmudrāṃ pradarśya ghaṇṭāpūjāṃ kuryāt.*"

(By showing the symbolic gesture of ringing a bell, one should worship the bell.)

He is reciting a part of ritual instructions, not a *mantra.* cf. Fig. 49.

Fig. 40 The priest is showing the gesture (*mudrā*) of ringing a bell. It is only in this step that a symbolic gesture is used.

(8) *Consecration of the Lamp (Dīpapūjana)*

Purification of ritual utensils and materials occurs during steps A-7 and 8. After the water in the large pot has been consecrated, it acquires the same value as that of the sacred Ganges.

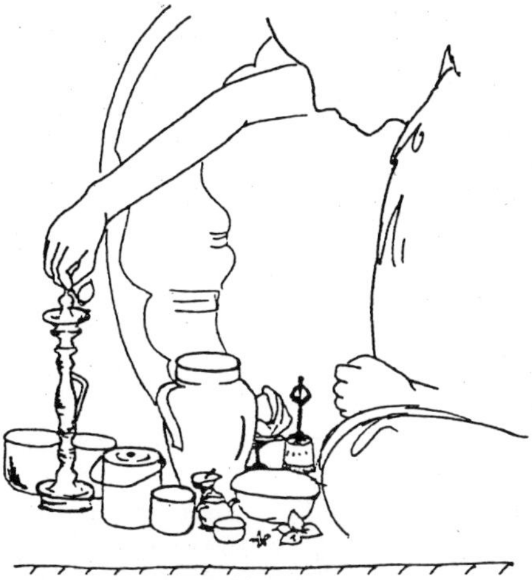

Fig. 41 The priest is consecrating the lamp by lighting it.

(9) *Consecration of Self and Materials for worship by Sprinkling Water (Prokṣaṇa)*

The priest begins to recite the following purifying formula (*prokṣaṇamantra*): *apavitraḥ pavitraḥ vā sarvāvasthāṃ gato 'pi vā/ yaḥ*

Fig. 42 The priest is dipping out some water. cf. Fig. 50.

smaret puṇḍarīkākṣaṃ sa bāhyābhyantaraḥ ściḥ// (No matter whether man is pure or impure, no matter what kind of state man has reached, if he remembers the Lotus-Eyed One, he will be purified within and without).

Then he says, "Having purified oneself, one should purify the materials for worship" (*ātmānaṃ prokṣya pūjādravyāṇi ca saṃprokṣet*).[17] While he is reciting the formula, he is sprinkling water on himself and on the materials for worship.

(B) Main worship

(1) *Invocation (Āvāhana) to the Goddess*

The Goddess is invoked.

"*sahasraśīrṣā puruṣaḥ sahasrākṣaḥ sahasrapāt/ sa bhūmiṃ viśvato vṛtvāty atiṣṭhad daśāṅgukam*"//1//[18]

"Puruṣa has a thousand heads, a thousand eyes, a thousand feet. On every side enveloping the earth, he overpassed [it] by a space of ten fingers."[19]

Fig. 43 The main worship now begins. The first five *upacāras* are performed within a half minute, while it takes more than one hour to finish the entire ritual. The first step is to invoke the deity. Here the invocation is done by means of incense. In this illustration the priest is lighting the incense.

17. cf. [Kane 1974: 739].
18. The Sanskrit text of the *Puruṣasūkta* is taken from [Aufrecht 1968 : Vol. 2, 387-8]. In this book the accents of Sanskrit words are deleted.
19. The English translation is taken from [Muir 1967: 9-11].

"*mahākālīdevatābhyo namaḥ. āvāhanaṃ samarpayāmi.*"
(Salutation to Goddess Mahākālī. I invoke [you, O Goddess].[20]

Fig. 44 He then fixes the incense in front of him.

(2) *Offering the Seat (Āsana) to the Goddess*

Fig. 45 The performing priest puts a small leaf of Tulasī (*Ocimum sanctum*) in a basin.

20. In the summer of 1982 it was said, "Salutation to Goddess Mahākālī, Mahālakṣmī, and Sarasvatī" (*mahākālīmahālakṣmīsarasvatīdevatābhyo namaḥ*). This expression was repeated after the recitation of each verse of the *Puruṣasūkta*.

The seat is offered to the goddess.

"puruṣa evedaṃ sarvaṃ yad bhūtaṃ yac ca bhavyam/ utāmṛtatvasyeśāno yad annenātirohati"//2//

(Puruṣa himself is this whole [universe], whatever has been and whatever shall be. He is also the lord of immortality, since [or, when] by food he expands.)

"mahākālīdevatābhyo namaḥ. tulasīpatraṃ samarpayāmi."

(Salutation to Goddess Mahākālī. I offer [you] a Tulasī leaf [for your seat].) Here Catuḥśṛṅgī is called Mahākālī.

(3) *Offering the Water for Washing the Feet (Pādya) of the Goddess*

The water for washing the feet of the goddess is offered.

"etāvān asya mahimāto jyāyāṅś ca pūruṣaḥ/ pādo 'sya viśvā bhūtāni tripād asyāmṛtaṃ divi" //3//

(Such is his greatness, and Puruṣa is superior to this. All existences are a quarter of him; and three-fourths of him are that which is immortal in the sky.)

"mahākālīdevatābhyo namaḥ. pādayoḥ pādyaṃ samarpayāmi."

(Salutation to Goddess Mahākālī. I offer [you]the water to wash your feet.)[21]

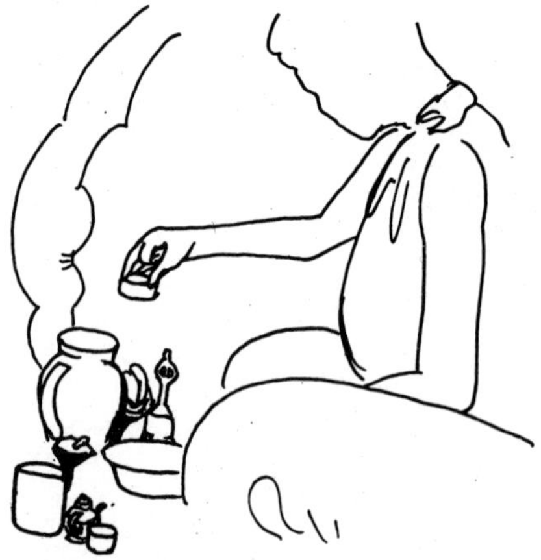

Fig. 46 The priest takes a small bowl (Fig. 36(8)) filled with water and places it near the image of the goddess.

21. cf. [Gonda 1976: 77], [Johnston 1972: 5 (I-52)] [Kane 1974: 727].

(4) *Offering the Sacred Water (Arghya)*

The sacred water is offered.

> "*tripād ūrdhva ud ait puruṣaḥ pādo 'syehābhavat punaḥ/ tato vishvañ vy akrāmat sāśa nānaśane abhi*" //4//
>
> (With three quarters Puruṣa mounted upwards. A quarter of him was again produced here. He was then diffused everywhere over things which eat and things which do not eat.)
>
> "*mahākālīdevatābhyo namaḥ. hastayoḥ arghyaṃ samarpayāmi.*"
>
> (Salutation to Goddess Mahākālī. I offer [you] the sacred water for [your] hands.)

Arghya is the sacred water offered to the deity. Here the priest takes another bowl (Fig. 36(9)) filled with water and places it closer to the image of the goddess than the first one.

(5) *Offering the Water for Rinsing the Mouth (Ācamanīya)*

The water for rinsing the mouth is offered.

> "*tasmād virāḷ ajāyata virājo adhi pūruṣaḥ/ sa jāto aty aricyata paścād bhūmim atho puraḥ*" //5//
>
> (From him was born Virāj, and from Virāj, Puruṣa. When born, he extended beyond the earth, both behind and before.)
>
> "*mahākālīdevatābhyo namaḥ. ācamanīyaṃ samarpayāmi.*"
>
> (Salutation to Goddess Mahākālī. I offer [you]the water for rinsing [your mouth].)[22]

Fig. 47 The priest is about to take a bowl filled with water. This bowl is larger than that used for the *arghya* water.

22. cf. [Joshi n.d. b: 17].

(6) *Purification of the Deity by Bathing* (*Snāna*)

Now he is going to bathe the image of Goddess Catḥśṛṅgī with the five ambrosia (*pañcāmṛita*): milk, curds, ghee (clarified butter), honey, and sugar. Then he consecrates the goddess with water. This step (B-6) is the most important of the sixteen 'ways of worshipping' (*upacāra*), and it takes about half an hour.

> "*yat puruṣeṇa haviṣā devā yajñam atanvata/ vasanto asyāsīd ājyaṃ grīṣma idhmaḥ śarad dhaviḥ*" //6//
>
> (When the gods performed a sacrifice with Puruṣa as the oblation, the spring was its butter, the summer its fuel, and the autumn its [accompanying] offering.)
>
> "*mahākālīdevatābhyo namaḥ. snānaṃ samarpayāmi.*"
>
> (Salutation to Goddess Mahākālī. I offer to bathe you.)[23]

Each time one of the five ambrosia is offered, a verse of the *Ṛgveda* is recited.

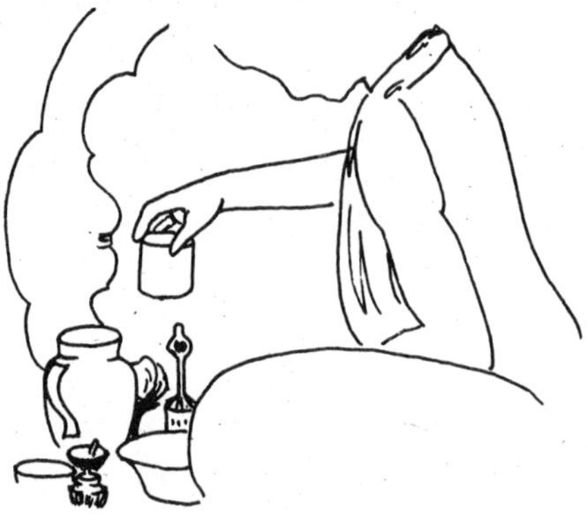

Fig. 48 The priest is placing the milk-pot near the image of Goddess Catuḥśṛṅgī.

(a) Bathing with Milk (*Payas*)

Ṛgveda (I, 91, 16) is recited. In this verse the term "*soma*" (the juice of the *soma* plant) refers to milk (*payas*).

> "Increase, Soma. May vigour come to thee from every side. Be diligent in the supply of food [to us]."[24]

---

23. cf. [Joshi n.d. b: 18], [Kane 1974: 739].
24. [Wilson 1977: Vol. 1, 234].

Fig. 49 Milk is spreading over the head of the goddess. "*śuddhodaka-snānaṃ samarpayāmi.*" (I offer [you] a bath of pure water.)

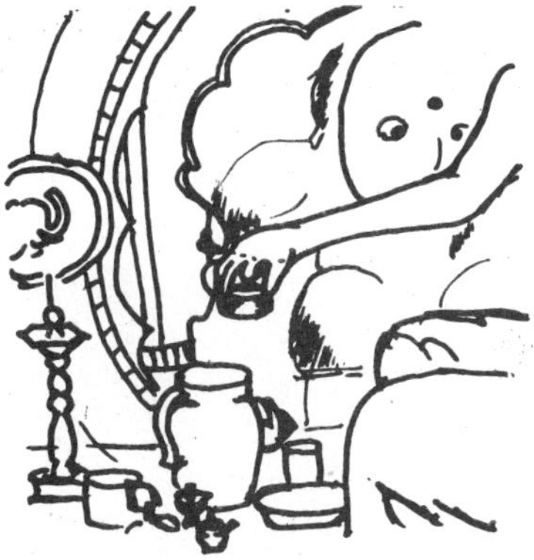

Fig. 50 He takes a bowl filled with water. He is going to pour the water over the head of the Goddess.

(b) Bathing with Curds (*Dadhi*)

Ṛgveda (IV, 39, 6) is recited.[25] In this verse the letters "*dadhi*" appear, although they do not here signify curds.

> "I have celebrated the praise of Dadhikra, the rapid and victorious steed: may he make our mouths fragrant, may he prolong our lives."[26]

25. cf. [Joshi n.d. b: 19].
26. [Wilson 1977: Vol. 3, 198].

Fig. 51 The curd which have spread over the head of the goddess is being washed away by water.

(c) Bathing with Ghee (*Ghṛta*)

Ṛgveda (II, 3, 11) is recited. In this verse the term "*ghṛta*" (ghee, [clarified] butter) appears.

Fig. 52 The ghee which has been spread over the face of the goddess is to be washed away with water as in the previous cases. It seems that at this stage the performing priest is using the curd mixed with ghee.

"I sprinkle the butter, for butter is his birthplace; he is nourished by butter; butter is his radiance : Agni, showerer [of benefits], bring the gods to the offered oblation; exhilarate them; convey to them the offering that has been reverently sanctified."[27]

(d) Bathing with Honey (*Madhu*)

Ṛgveda (I, 90, 6) is recited. In this verse the term "*madhu*" (honey, sweet) is repeated.

> "The winds bring sweet [rewards] to the sacrificer; the rivers bring sweet [water]. May the herbs yield sweetness to us."[28]

Fig. 53 The priest is holding a small cup filled with honey water.

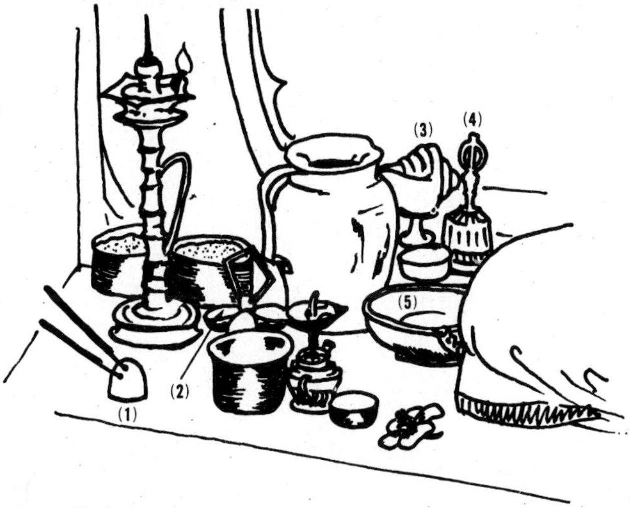

Fig. 54 (1) incense stand (cf. Fig. 44), (2) the small vessel for *kuṃkuma* and *haridrā* (cf. Fig. 36(3)), (3) conch (cf. Fig. 39), (4) bell, (5) basin (cf. Fig. 45)

27. [Wilson 1977: Vol. 2, 219].
28. [Wilson 1977: Vol. 1, 231].

(e) Bathing with Water Mixed with Sugar (*Śarkara*)

Ṛgveda (IX, 85, 6) is recited. In this verse the word "*svādu*" (sweet) refers to sugar (*śarkara*).[29]

> "Flow sweet for the celestial people, flow sweet for Indra, whose name is worthily invoked; sweet for Mitra, Varuṇa, Vāyu, Bṛihaspati, thou who art sweet-flavoured, inviolable."[30]

Fig. 55 The priest is taking a small quantity of sugar or saccharin out of the sugar-bottle.

(f) Bathing with Fragrant Water (*Gandhodaka*)

Fig. 56 The priest puts a small white flower into the bowl in which sugar had already been placed. Now he is pouring water into the bowl. He is going to pour the sweet and fragrant water on the goddess. It seems that B–6–(e) and B–6–(f) are done at the same time.

29. cf. [Joshi n.d. b: 19].
30. [Wilson 1977: Vol. 6, 340].

(i) *Anointing with Yellow Powder* (*Haridrā*) *and Red Powder* (*Kuṃkuma*)

Fig. 57 The priest will anoint with yellow powder and red powder again in the ninth step (B–9). cf. Fig. 67.

(ii) *Offering Flowers* (*Puṣpa*)

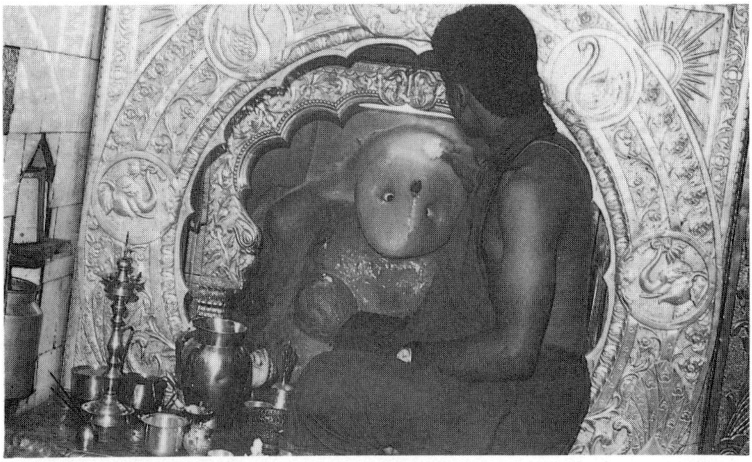

Fig. 58 A white Champak flower is being placed on the head of the goddess.

(g) Offering the Lamp (*Dīpa*)

Here no Vedic *mantra* is recited.

Fig. 59 The performing priest is lighting a small lamp. He is going to put it between the stand (Fig. 36(1)) and the pot (Fig. 36(5)).

(h) Consecration (*Abhiṣeka*)

The priest is going to consecrate the sacred image of the goddess by sprinkling water. Consecration is done by means of a pot filled with water, which is hung above the head of the image of the goddess.

> *"uttare nirmālyaṃ visṛjya abhiṣekaṃ kuryāt."*
>
> (Having moved to the northern corner [of the sanctuary] the things previously offered, one should consecrate [the goddess] by water.)

Fig. 60 He is hanging the pot above the goddess.

(i) *Consecration with the Recitation of Puruṣasūkta* (*Ṛgveda*, X, 90, 1-16)

The priests have recited each verse of *Puruṣasūkta* at each of the sixteen steps (*upacāra*). Now the sixth step is being performed, and the priests are going to recite the entire *Puruṣasūkta* without stopping.

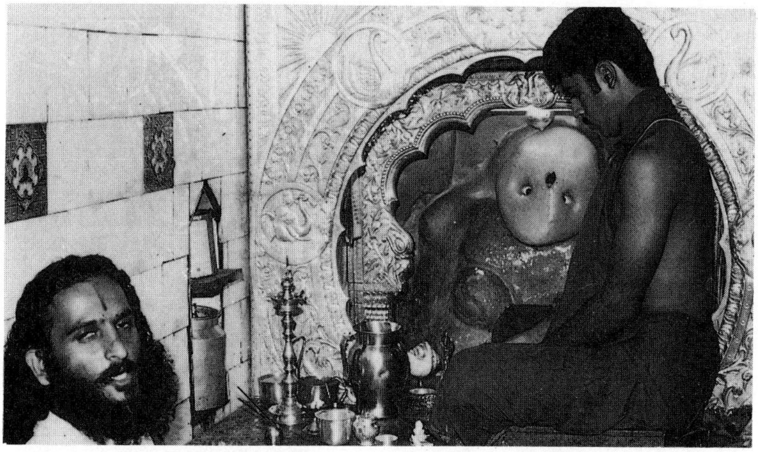

Fig. 61 Drops of water fall from a small hole in the bottom of the consecration pot.

(ii) *Consecration with the Recitation of Śrīsūkta* (*Ṛgveda*, V, 87)

Both priests recite *Śrīsūkta* sixteen times.[31] While they are reciting it, they do not perform any special action.

(iii) *Consecration with the Recitation of Rudra* (*Kṛṣṇa Yajurveda*, IV, 5, 1–11)[32]

(iv) *Consecration with the Recitation of Vasor Dhārā* (*Kṛṣṇa Yajurveda*, IV, 7, 1–11)[33]

---

31. cf. [Aufrecht 1968: Vol. 2, 674], [Macdonell 1965: 189], [Sontakke & Kashikar 1946: 927–930].
32. cf. [Apte 1948:2001], [Keith 1914: 353].
33. cf. [Apte 1948: 2078–2091], [Keith 1914: 380].

Fig. 62 As soon as the consecration pot became empty, the priest filled it again with water and hung it again above the goddess. *Vasor dhārā* is still being recited.

Fig. 63 Having taken the conch filled with water, the priest is pouring the water on the head of the goddess. The consecration pot has been taken off.

(7) *Offering the Garment* (*Vastra*)

The garment is offered to the goddess.

> "*taṃ yajñaṃ barhiṣi praukṣan puruṣaṃ jātam agrataḥ/ tena devā ayajanta sādhyā ṛṣayaś ca ye*"//7//
>
> (This victim, Puruṣa, born in the beginning, they immolated on the sacrificial grass. With him the gods, the Sādhyas, and the Ṛṣis sacrificed.)

"*mahākālīdevatābhyo namaḥ. vastraṃ samarpayāmi.*"
(Salutation to Goddess Mahākālī. I offer [you] a garment.)

Fig. 64

(8) *Offering the Upper Garment* (*Upavastra*)

The upper garment is offered.

"*tasmād yajñāt sarvahutaḥ sambhṛtaṃ pṛṣad ājyam/ paśūn tāṅś cakre vāyavyān āraṇyān grāmyāś ca ye*" //8//

(From that universal sacrifice were provided curds and butter. It formed those aerial [creatures] and animals both wild and tame.)

"*mahākālīdevatābhyo namaḥ. upavastraṃ samarpayāmi.*"

Fig. 65

(Salutation to Goddess Mahākālī. I offer [you] an upper garment.)[34]

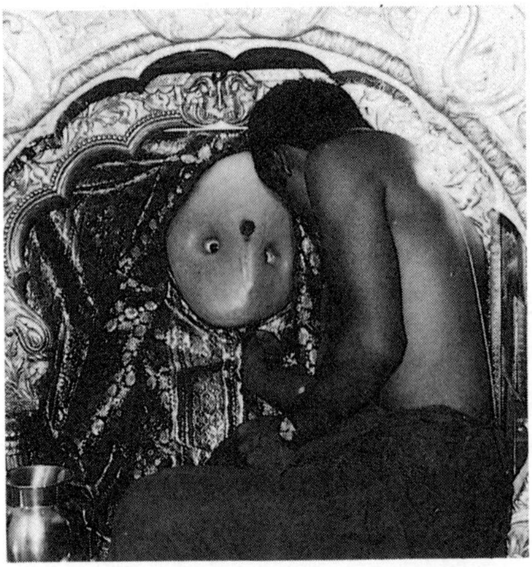

Fig. 66 The priest has almost finished putting on the upper garment.

(9) *Offering Fragrant Materials (Gandha)*

Fig. 67 The priest is putting the *kuṃkuma* paste on the upper part of the forehead of the goddess and the *haridrā* paste on the lower part. cf. B–6–f(i).

34. cf. [Joshi n.d. b:21].

Fragrant materials are offered.

> "*tasmād yajñāt sarvahuta ṛcaḥ sāmāni jajñire/ chandāṅsi jajñire tasmād yajus tasmād ajāyata*" //9//
> (From that universal sacrifice sprang the rich and *sāman* verse, the metres, and the *yajus.*)
> "*mahākālīdevatābhyo namaḥ. kuṃkumaṃ samarpayāmi.... haridrāṃ samarpayāmi.*"

Fig. 68 He is offering flowers of Hibiscus and Niśigandha.

Fig. 69 The performing priest is now putting a necklace on the goddess. The priest's mother came and sat in the place of the prompting priest, who moved to the right side of the sanctuary.

(Salutation to Goddess Mahākālī. I offer [you] *kuṃkuma.* ... I offer [you] *haridrā.*)[35]

(10) *Offering Flowers* (*Puṣpa*)

Fig. 70 He has almost finished adorning the goddess.

Fig. 71 At this moment the prompting priest left the main hall of the temple in order to bring some material, and the *pūjā* stopped for fifteen minutes.

35. cf. [Joshi n.d. b: 21].

Flowers are offered.

> "*tasmād aśvā ajāyanta ye ke cobhayādataḥ/ gāvo ha jajñire tasmāt tasmāj jātā ajāvayaḥ*" //10//
> (From it sprang horses, and all animals with two rows of teeth; kine sprang from it; from it goats and sheep.)
> "*mahākālīdevatābhyo namaḥ. puṣpāṇi samarpayāmi.*"
> (Salutation to Goddess Mahākālī. I offer [you] flowers.)

(11) Offering Incense (*Dhūpa*)

Incense is offered.

> "*yat puruṣaṃ vy adadhuḥ katidhā vy akalpayan/ mukhaṃ kim asya kau bāhū kā ūrū pādā ucyete*"//11//
> (When [the gods] divided Puruṣa, into how many parts did they cut him up? What was his mouth? What arms [had he]? What [two objects] are said [to have been] his thighs and feet)?
> "*mahākālīdevatābhyo namaḥ. dhūpaṃ samarpayāmi.*"
> (Salutation to Goddess Mahākālī. I offer incense.)[36]

Fig. 72 The performing priest has finished adorning the goddess. The *Ṣoḍaśa-upacāra-pūjā* is almost over. He is now lighting incense. The prompting priest has come back and is now sitting at the entrance to the sanctuary.

36. cf. [Joshi n.d. b: 22].

(12) *Offering the Lamp (Dīpa) and Fragrant Materials (Gandha)*

"*brāhmaṇo 'sya mukham āsīd bāhū rājanyaḥ kṛtaḥ/ ūrū tad asya yad vaiśyaḥ padbhyāṃ śūdro ajāyata*" //12//
(The Brāhman wash his mouth; the Rājanya was made his thighs and arms; the being [called] the Vaiśya, he was his thighs; the Sūdra sprang from his feet.)
"*mahākālīdevatābhyo namaḥ. dīpaṃ samarpayāmi.*"
(Salutation to Goddess Mahākālī. I offer [you] a lamp.)

Fig. 73

(13) *Offering Food (Naivedya)*

"*candramā manaso jātaś cakṣoḥ sūryo ajāyata/ mukhād indraś cāgniś ca prāṇād vāyur ajāyata*" //13//
(The moon sprang from his soul (*menas*), the sun from his eye, Indra and Agni from his mouth, and Vāyu from his breath.)
"*mahākālīdevatābhyo namaḥ naivedyaṃ samarpayāmi.*"[37]
(Salutation to Goddess Mahākālī. I offer [you] food.)

The *naivedya* offering consists of fruits and milk, if the worship service is performed in the evening and morning. The *naivedya* offering for the mid-day *pūjā* consists of daily meals in the noon.[38]

37. cf. [Joshi n.d. b: 23].
38. cf. [Kane 1974: 733].

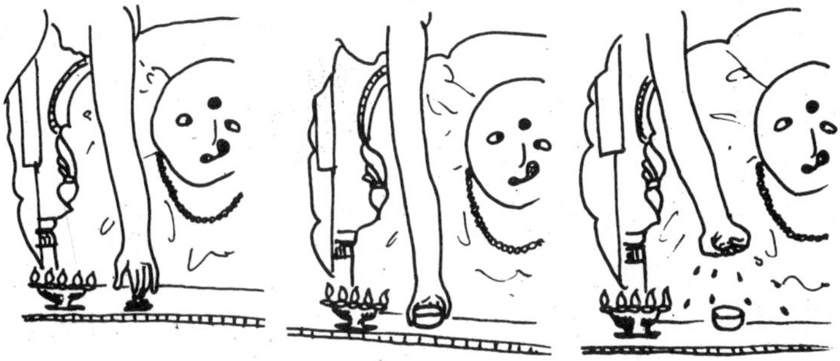

Fig. 74 Fig. 75 Fig. 76

First the priest anoints the altar with water (Fig. 74.). Then he places a small cup filled with food (*naivedya*) on the anointed or consecrated spot (Fig. 75). Finally he sprinkles it over the food (Fig. 76).

Fig. 77 He has just finished offering food.

The five substances, i.e., milk, curds, ghee, honey, and sugar, which are offered at the sixth stage of *Ṣoḍaśa-upacāra-pūjā* (cf. B-6) are also called the *naivedya* offering.

(14) *Circling the Deity Clockwise* (*Pradakṣiṇā*) *and Waving the Lamp* (*Ārātrika*)

The fourteenth step in the *pradakṣiṇā* (clockwise circling of the sacred image).[39] If there is no space to do the *pradakṣiṇā*, the priest is supposed to turn his own body round. In this worship service, however, the priest did not perform the *pradakṣiṇā*. The priest did perform the *pradakṣiṇā* however, when *mahāpūjā* (an elaborate form of *Ṣoḍaśa-upacāra-pūjā*) was conducted on July 25, 1979 at same the temple. At that time, another Angal family was in charge of this temple.

"*nābhyā āsīd antarikṣaṃ śīrṣṇo dyauḥ sam avartata/ padbhyāṃ bhūmir diśaḥ śrotrāt tathā lokāñ akalpayan*" //14//
(From his navel arose the air, from his head the sky, from his feet the earth, from his ear the [four] quarters: in this manner [the gods] formed the worlds.)
"*mahākālīdevatābhyo namaḥ. pradakṣiṇāṃ samarpayāmi.*"
(Salutation to Goddess Mahākālī. I offer [you] *pradakṣiṇā*.)

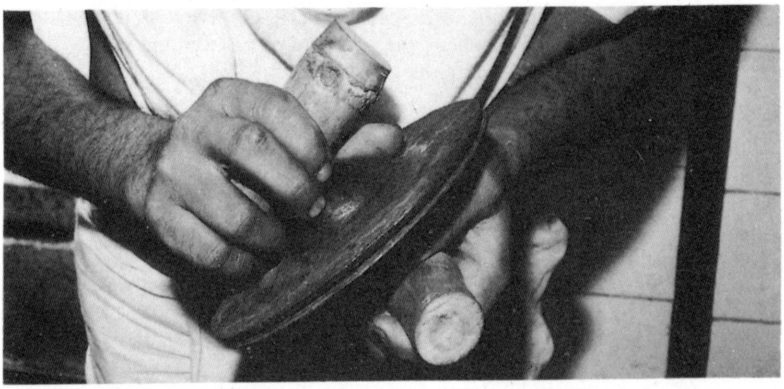

Fig. 78 Making sounds with symbals, a man is felicitating the goddess who has manifested herself in her complete form.

39. The following photographs (*a* and *b*) show the priests performing a *mahāpūjā* on July 25, 1979, at Catiḥśṛṅgī Temple. In *a*, one can see priests standing and ringing symbals and bells. In *b*, the priests can be seen performing *pradakṣiṇā* (circling the deity clockwise). They are not circling the sacred image clockwise, but they are moving clockwise in front of the goddess. cf. [Aiyangar 1940: 8, 25; 30; 59].

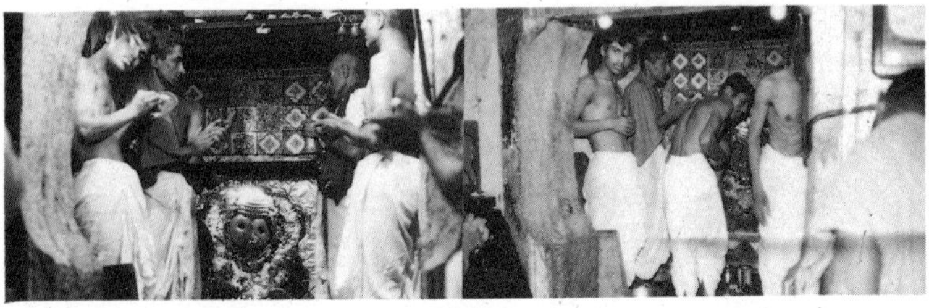

a b

Fig. 79 Having lit the lamp on the right side of the sanctuary, the priest is beginning to wave the *ārātrika* lamp. His mother is standing on the right. (The cat is not involved in the ritual.)

Fig. 80 Three men are ringing bells in the western half of the main hall. The entire time the priest is waving the lamp.

The *ārātrika* lamp held in the right hand of the priest kept moving in circles. At first it moved in a circle counterclockwise, then clockwise. The motion lasted for about five minutes. The priest was standing in the same place until the waving of the *ārātrika* lamp was finished. Although the waving of the lamp is not counted as a step of the *Ṣoḍaśa-upacāra-pūjā*, it has become the climax of this ritual.

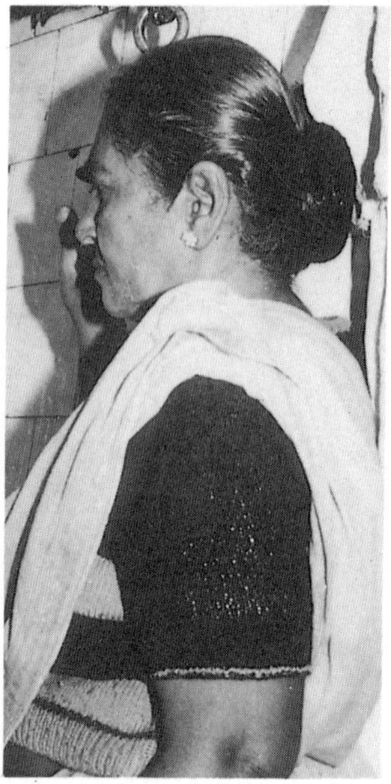

Fig. 81 The mother of the performing priest is ringing the bell which is hung from the ceiling.

(15) *Salutation (Namaskāra)*

Here the priests salute the goddess with their hands joined. See Figs. 106, 107, and 125.

"*saptāsyāsan paridhayas triḥ sapta samidhaḥ kṛtāḥ/ devā yad yajñaṃ tanvānā abadhnan puruṣaṃ paśum*"//15//
(When the gods, performing sacrifice, bound Puruṣa as a victim, there were seven sticks [stuck up] for it [around the fire], and thrice seven pieces of fuel were made.)
"*mahākālīdevatābhyo namaḥ. namaskāraṃ samarpayāmi.*"
(Salutation to Goddess Mahākālī. I offer [you] salutation.)

(16) *Offering Flowers with the Recitation of Mantra (Mantrapuṣpa)*

"*yajñena yajñam ayajanta devās tāni dharmāṇi prathamāny āsan/ te ha nākaṃ mahimānaḥ sacanta yatra pūrve sādhyāḥ santi devāḥ*" //16//

(With sacrifice the gods performed the sacrifice. These were the earliest rites. These great powers have sought the sky, where are the former Sādhyas, gods.)

"mahākālīdevatābhyo namaḥ. mantrapuṣpaṃ samarpayāmi."
(Salutation to Goddess Mahākālī. I offer [you] flowers and formulae.)

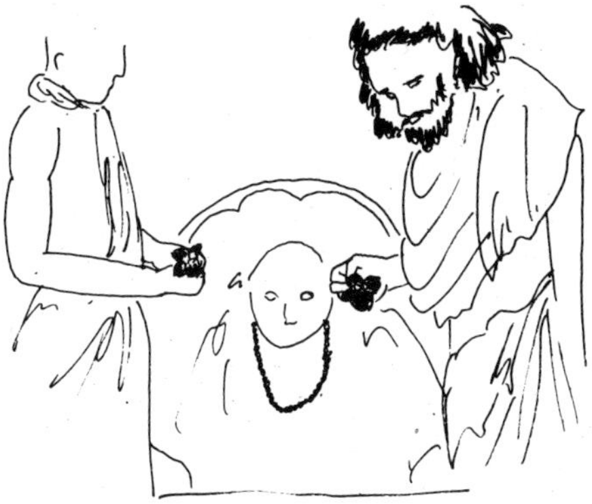

Fig. 82 Both of the priests are going to throw flowers towards the goddess while reciting *mantras*.[40] The *pūjā* is now finished.

Fig. 83 The image of Goddess Catuḥśṛṅgī.

40. cf. [Joshi n.d. b: 24].

Obtaining Power from Goddess Catuḥśṛṅgī

Here the *pūjā* has been finished. There remains, however, one more part, which is especially important to patrons or devotees. The people, having watched or attended the *pūjā*, come up to the priest and are given the *prasāda*, i.e., blessing or the remnants of the food offered to the divine image. Obtaining the *prasāda* is one of the main purposes of those who come to temples.

Fig. 84 As soon as the *ārātrika* was over, the lamp was placed on the floor.

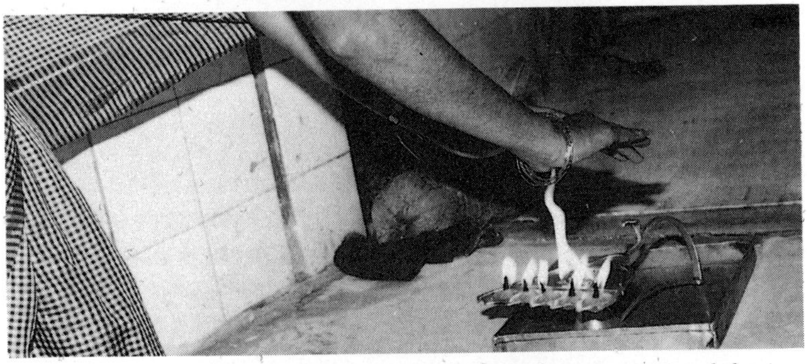

Fig. 85 This lady puts her hands over the lamp for a moment and then touches her body with her hands.[41] This kind of action is believed to be one way to obtain divine power.

---

41. The Hindu lady in this picture was helping me take records of the worship. Although she is not particularly devoted to Goddess Catuḥśṛṅgī, she did this action very smoothly and quickly.

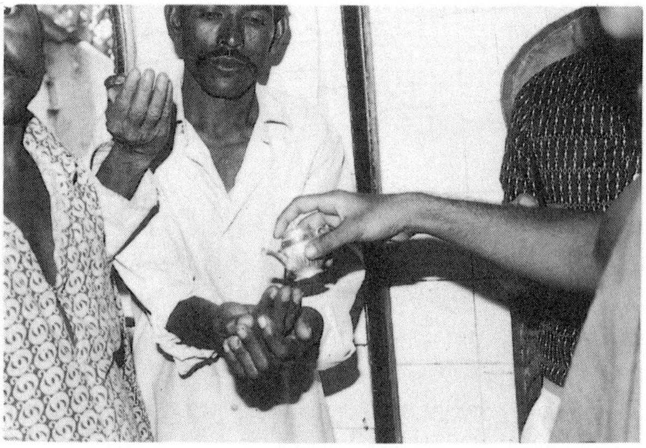

Fig. 86 Consecrated water is given to people by the priest. For the pot of holy water, see Fig. 36(7).

Then the priest gives them a piece of coconut as *prasāda* or a gift in token of their offering. Some of them belong to the trustees of this temple, and others have been employed to ring bells.

Fig. 87 This lady came into the main hall about ten minutes before the worship was finished. She is devoted to Goddess Catuḥśṛṅgī. She is about to offer a coconut, a green cloth (*khaṇ*), and flowers to Goddess Catuḥśṛṅgī. cf. Fig. 8.

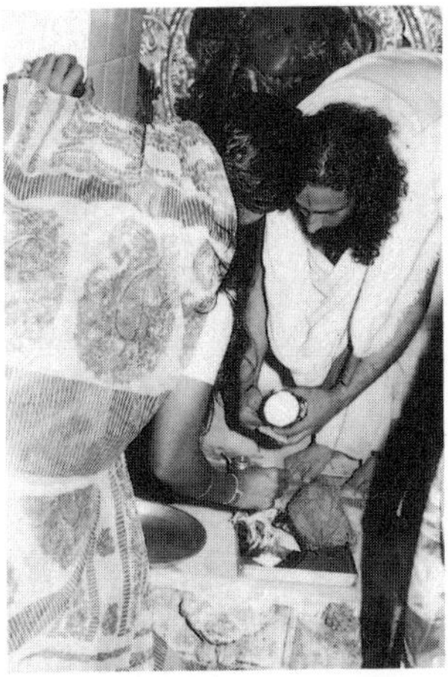

Fig. 88 Here she is receiving a piece of coconut as *prasāda*.

Appendix I

ṢOḌAŚA-UPACĀRA-PŪJĀ AT NĀGEŚVAR TEMPLE, POONA

The following photos in Appendix I show the general procedure of the *Ṣoḍaśa-upacāra-pūjā* performed at Nāgeśvar Temple, Somavar Peth, Poona, on the night of August 22, 1981. This temple is a Viṣṇu temple, and Somavar Peth is an area of old Poona. The worship service was performed for Vittal and Rukmiṇī, who are, respectively, an incarnation of Viṣṇu and his wife. Although the main deities of the worship performed at Nāgeśvar Temple differed from the deity of the worship at Catuḥśṛṅgī Temple, which we have seen in the previous section on Catuḥśṛṅgī Temple, the general procedure of these two *pūjās* was almost the same. The *Ṣoḍaśa-upacāra-pūjā* thus furnishes one of the basic norms of Hindu worship services. Yet there were some differences in the manner of worship in these two *pūjās*. One of the most remarkable differences between them was that the patron (*yajamāna*) participated in the worship performed at Nāgeśvar Temple, whereas in Catuḥśṛṅgī Temple the performing priest himself carried out all the ritual actions. Also, devotees can enter the sanctuary of the former, but no one except a member of the Angal family is entitled to enter the sanctuary of the latter.

The patron of the worship service performed at Nāgeśvar Temple is a medical doctor who lives near the temple. The worship was conducted by a priest and his son belonging to the Vaiṣṇava School. The worship started at 9:38 P.M. and ended at 10:18 P.M.

Nāgeśvar Temple also functions as an Āśrama (church) for those who belong to Kāṇvaśākhā, i.e., a branch of the White Yajur Veda School, which is closely associated with the Vittal cult. On the night when the worship was performed at this temple, there was a festival of Kāṇvaśākhā people in the main hall of the same temple.[42]

42. I would like to thank Mr. Manjul (Library of Bhandarkar Institute, Poona) who enabled me and Mr. Hori to take photographs of the *pūjā* in the sanctuary of Nāgeśvar Temple. In Vittal Temples, such as Nāgeśvar, laymen can enter the sanctum.

Fig. 89 The *pūjā* (worship) is going to be performed in the sanctuary, from which a lady is here seen emerging.

Fig. 90 Images of Vittal and Rukmiṇī are seen on the altar found in the sanctuary.

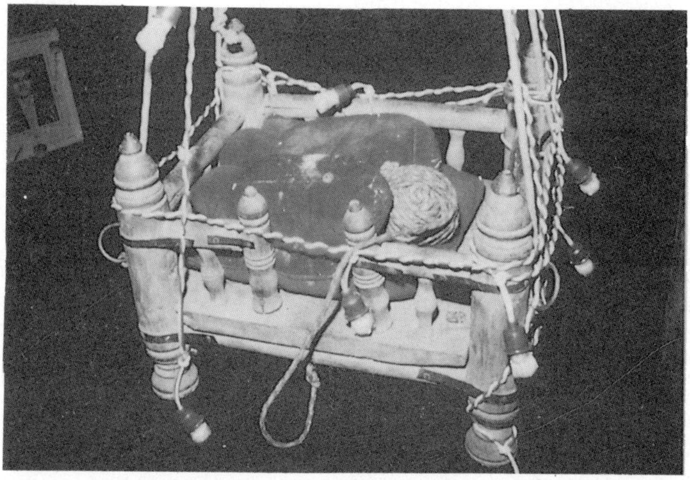

Fig. 91 The 22nd of August, 1981, was the birthday of Kṛṣṇa. A tiny image of Baby Kṛṣṇa is found in a small cradle hung from the ceiling.

Fig. 92 These are materials used for worshipping the divinities.

Fig. 93 The priest (left) tells the patron and his wife that the *pūjā* is about to begin.

Fig. 94 The garments covering the deities have been taken off so that the deities can be bathed.

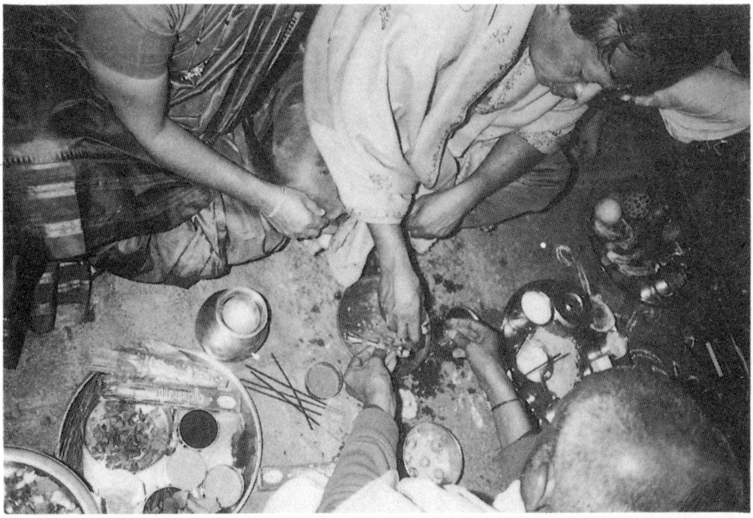

Fig. 95 The patron (*yajamāna*) is preparing the offerings to the divinities according to the instructions of the priest.

A~B–5. Preliminaries and the First Five Steps

Preliminaries (A–1~9) and the first five steps of the main worship (B–1~5) were performed almost in the same order as the worship at Catuḥśṛṅgī Temple. The actions representing those steps were, however, not distinguishable from each other, mainly because the worship was mostly performed by the patron and his wife. Here in Appendix I, I will include only those photographs representing several steps in the latter half of the worship, i.e., B–6~15. It is interesting to note that in this service the wife of the patron made an offering to the deity with her hands and adorned the image of the deity with garments and flower garlands. In the worship performed at Pārvatī Nandana Temple, the wife of a householder, as we shall see in Appendix II, does not have the right to touch the image of the deity directly with her hand.

B–6. *Purification of the Deity by Bathing (Snāna)*

B–6–(b) Bathing with Curds (*Dadhi*)

Fig. 96 The patron is about to take the bowl filled with curds.

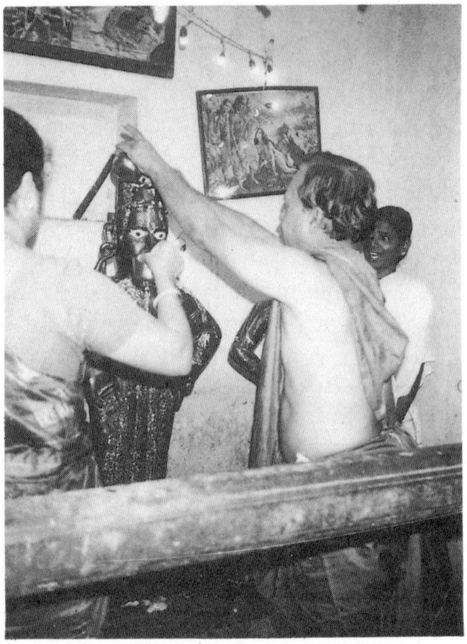

Fig. 97 They are pouring curd on the head of Vittal.

Fig. 98 The curds, milk, etc., which were poured on the images, have been washed away with water. The bathing (*snāna*) process was over.

B–7. *Offering the Garment* (*Vastra*)

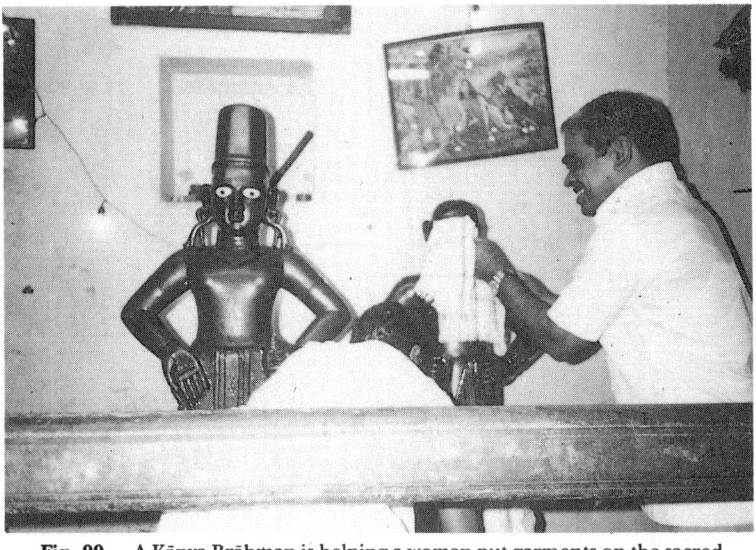

Fig. 99 A Kāṇva Brāhman is helping a woman put garments on the sacred images.

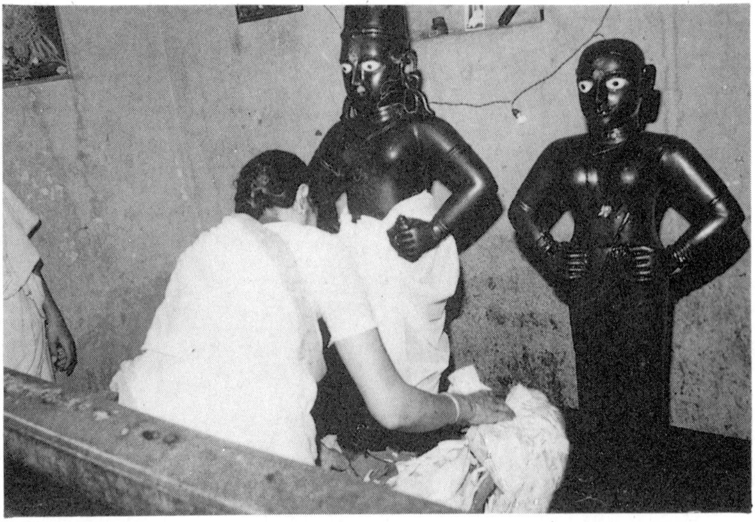

Fig. 100 This woman also belongs to the Kāṇva branch.

B–8. *Offering the Upper Garment* (*Upavastra*)

Fig. 101 The upper garment (*upavastra*) of Vittal is being put on.

B–9. *Offering Fragrant Materials* (*Gandha*)

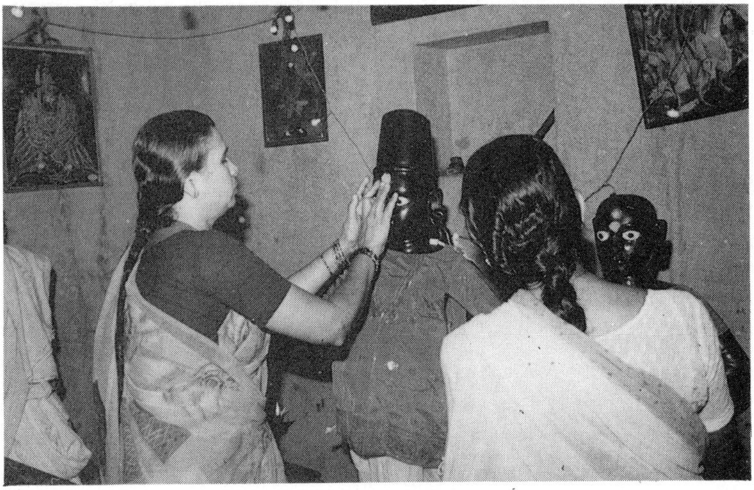

Fig. 102 *Kuṃkuma* paste is being put on the forehead of Vittal.

B–10. *Offering Flowers* (*Puṣpa*)

Fig. 103 A flower garland is being placed on Vittal by the patron. Then incense (B–11), the lamp and fragrant materials (B–12) are offered.

B–13. *Offering Food (Naivedya)*

Fig. 104 Fruit, sweets, curds, *tāmbūla,* etc., have been offered to the deities. cf. [Kane 1974: 734].

B–14. *Waving the Lamp (Ārātrika)*

Fig. 105 *Ārātrika* is performed by the patron and his wife, not by the priest. Flamable camphor is put on a large plate, which is then used as a waving (*ārtī*) lamp. They are moving the plate in a circle. (They did not circle the deity clockwise.)

B–15. *Salutation* (*Namaskāra*)

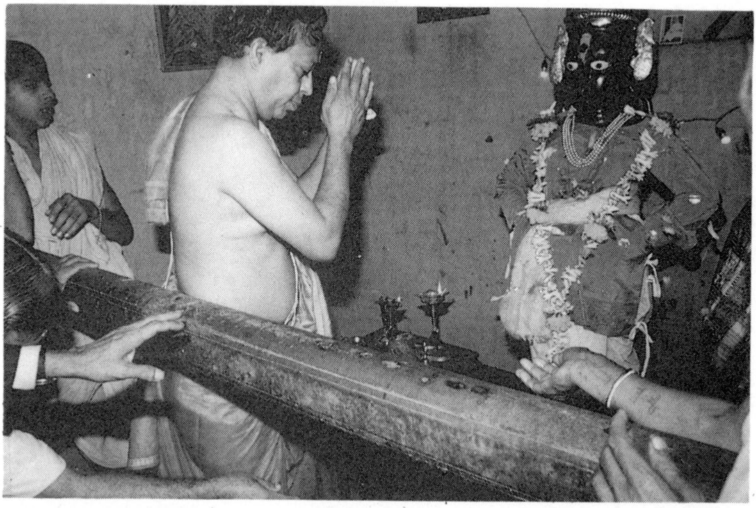

Fig. 107 His wife is doing *namaskāra.*

Appendix II

ṢOḌAŚA-UPACĀRA-PŪJĀ AT PĀRVATĪ NANDANA TEMPLE, POONA

Appendix II illustrates the general procedure of the *Ṣoḍaśa-upacāra-pūjā* performed at Pārvatī Nandana Temple, which is a Gaṇapati Temple, on the morning of January 14, 1982. The worship service was held for Gaṇapati, one of the most popular deities in the Poona district. A Brahman family, who live very close to Pārvatī Nandana Temple, performed the worship without the presence of any priest. The householder of the family conducted the worship. He recited the ritual text which consists of *mantras* and Vedic passages.[43]

Fig. 108 The *pūjā* is going to be performed in front of this image of God Gaṇapati.

43. I am very grateful to Mr. H. Hori, who allowed me to use the photographs in Appendix II of this book. I was not succesful in taking photographs of the first several steps of the worship service performed at Catuḥśṛṅgī Temple while I was staying in Poona in the summer of 1981. Therefore, I asked Mr. Hori, who was studying at the University of Poona, to take some photos of the earlier steps of a *Ṣoḍaśa-upacāra-pūjā*. In the spring of 1982 Mr. Hori sent me these photographs from Poona. I also wish to express my deepest gratitude to Mr. Manjul (Library of Bhandarkar Institute), who enabled Mr. Hori to have the chance to photograph the worship. Even though I was unable to observe the ritual, I have decided to use those photos in this book, for they clearly show the earlier steps, especially, A–1, 5, and 7, of Worship Service in Sixteen Steps. These steps are not so clearly illustrated in the section on Catuḥśṛṅgī Temple and Appendix I.

A. Preliminaries Performed by the Priest

A–1. *Purification of Self by Sipping Water* (*Ācamana*)

Fig. 109 The householder is purifying himself by sipping water (*ācamana*). When he performs a *pūjā*, his wife is supposed to accompany him. Her hands are visible on the left side of the photograph.

When he finishes purifying himself by sipping water, he controls his breath (A–2), recites Gāyatrīmantra (A–3), and contemplates the divinities (A–4).

A–5. *Declaration of Performance and Purpose* (*Saṃkalpa*)

No particular action representing the sixth preliminary step, i.e., worship of Gaṇapati (A–6) was observed. Here, however, all the preliminary steps (A–1~9) are considered to be worship of Gaṇapati.

Fig. 110 Looking at a calendar, he tells the exact time of the worship in astrological detail.

Fig. 111 This photograph shows the last part of A–5, i.e., declaration of performance and purpose. He is declaring the purpose of the worship.

A–7. *Consecration of the Pot, the Conch, and the Bell* (*Kalaśáśaṅkhaghaṇṭāpūjana*)

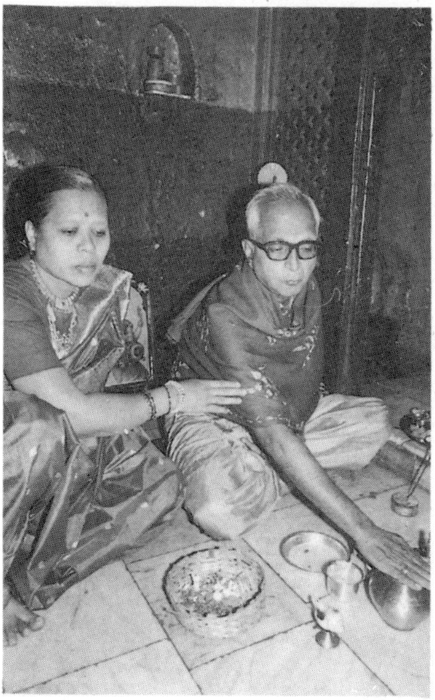

Fig. 112 He is consecrating the pot by touching its rim with his right hand. His wife is touching his right arm with her right hand. As she does not have the right to perform Worship Service in Sixteen Steps, this is the way she participates in this ritual.

Fig. 113 He is now consecrating the conch on a plate by dropping milk from a small ritual spoon.

Fig. 114 The bell is consecrated in the same way as the conch.

A–8. *Consecration of the Lamp* (*Dīpapūjana*)

The householder consecrates the lamp. Next the householder consecrates himself and the materials for worship by sprinkling them with water (*prokṣaṇa*) (A–9).

Fig. 115 Now the lamp is consecrated.

B. Main Worship

The main worship is to be performed according to the rules. (The photographs of the first five steps (B–1~5) could not be taken, since they were performed so quickly.)

B–6. *Purification of the Deity by Bathing* (*Snāna*)

B–6–(a) Bathing with Milk (*Payas*)

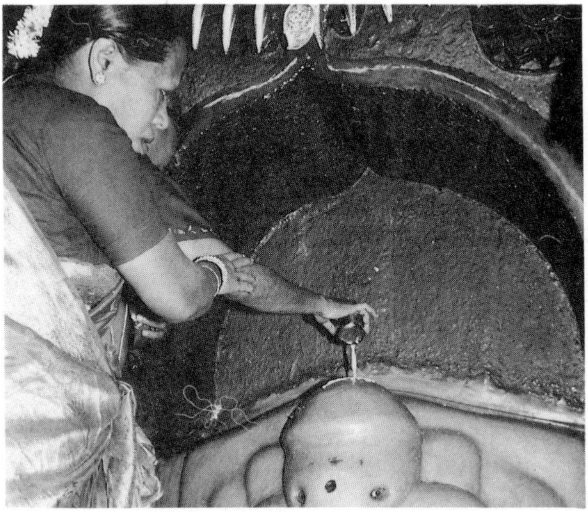

Fig. 116 The householder is pouring milk on the head of Gaṇapati, while his wife is touching his right arm.

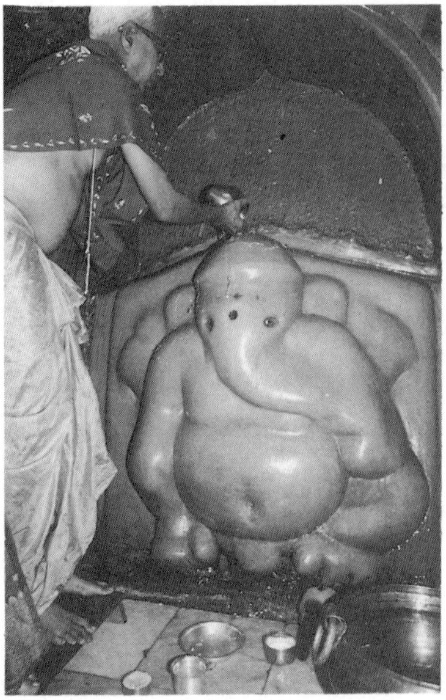

Fig. 117 The milk, which has been spread over Gaṇapati's head, is being washed away with water. Next, the householder bathes the deity with curds, ghee, honey, and the like (B–6–(a)~(f)).

B–6–f-(i) *Anointing with Red Powder* (*Kuṃkuma*)

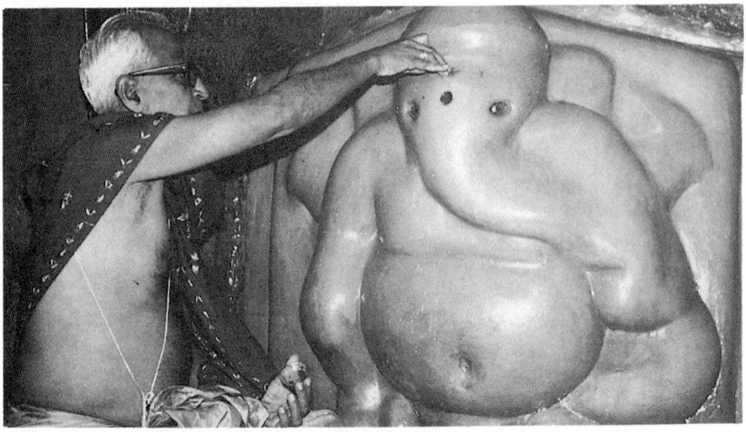

Fig. 118 He is putting red powder on Gaṇapati's forehead. His left hand is holding a small box of red powder. (No particular action representing step B–6–(g) was observed.)

B–6–(h) Consecration (*Abhiṣeka*)

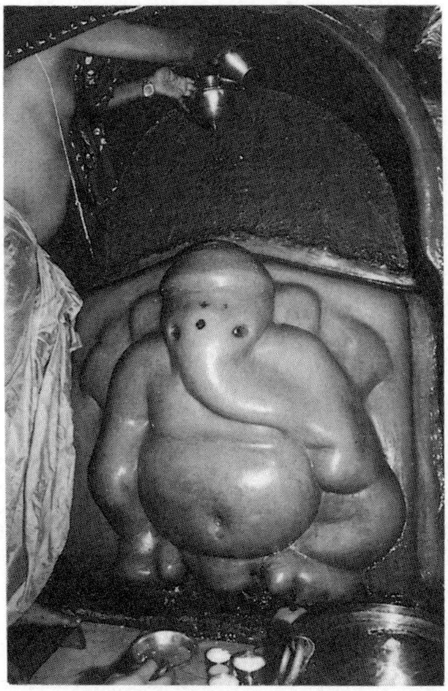

Fig. 119 A son of the householder is hanging a consecration pot (*abhiṣekapātra*) above Gaṇapati's head. As seen in Fig. 61, drops of water fall from a small hole in the bottom of the consecration pot.

B–7. *Offering the Garment* (*Vastra*)

Fig. 120 The son of the householder is putting a garment on the image of Gaṇapati.

B–8. *Offering the Upper Garment* (*Upavastra*)

B–9. *Offering Fragrant Materials* (*Gandha*)

B–10. *Offering Flowers* (*Puṣpa*)

Fig. 121 The upper garment, a necklace, a flower garland, and fragrant materials have been offered.

Then incense (*dhūpa*) (B–11) and the lamp (*dīpa*) (B–12) are offered.

B–13. *Offering Food* (*Naivedya*)

Fig. 122 He is dropping water from a small ritual spoon on the food such as fruits and betel nuts (*tāmbūla*). It is by this action that he offers food to Gaṇapati.

Fig. 123 Now that the householder has offered food, the rest of the family are offering food. The son is holding a plate filled with food, while his sister is touching him with her right hand in the same way as her mother does with her father. Her mother is standing behind her.

B–14. *Waving Lighted Candles* (*Ārātrika*)

Fig. 124 Circling the deity clockwise, which is the original fourteenth step (B–14), is not done. Instead, as in the case of the *Ṣoḍaśa-upacāra-pūjā* performed at Catuḥśṛṅgī Temple, 1981, they wave lighted candles (*ārātrika*). This photograph shows the householder who, by holding his right hand over the lighted candles, is trying to obtain divine power (cf. Fig. 85)

B–15. *Salutation* (*Namaskāra*)

Fig. 125 He is saluting Gaṇapati with his hands joined. Then he offers flowers with the recitation of *mantras* (B–16). The worship ends.

Appendix III

MAP OF POONA CITY

1. Catuḥśṛṅgī Temple; 2. Nāgeśvar Temple; 3. Pārvatī Nandana Temple; 4. Kasba Gaṇapati Temple; 5. Mhasobā Gate; 6. Mariai Gate; 7. University of Poona; 8. Bhandarkar Oriental Research Institute; 9. Deccan College; 10. Poona Station; 11. Mūlā River; 12. Muthā River; 13. Mūlā-Muthā River.

PART II

Sixteen Saṃskāras Handed Down by the Hiraṇyakeśins

Introduction

Hindu Saṃskāra is a popular ritualistic ceremony, expressive of the core of the Hindu religion. The sacraments relating to the body are called Saṃskāra rituals which aim at purifying the body, mind and intellect of an individual and are performed on all major stages of life from birth to death. The Saṃskāras cover the full span of life; they are performed even after the death of the individual.

A systematic treatment of the domestic rites is found in the Sūtra literature. The Gṛhyasūtras deal with the domestic rituals, which necessarily relate to the Saṃskāras. They give all the particulars of the relevant rituals and the Mantras that are to be recited during the performance of the Saṃskāras. The Gṛhyasūtras belong to different Vedic schools, and differ from one another to some extent.

The Prayoga 'practical handbook' and Paddhati 'guide-book or manual' texts which follow the Gṛhyasūtras are, of course, of a later date but their status cannot be ignored as an influencing force in relation to the performance of the Saṃskāras, as they present the Saṃskāras in greater details while the Gṛhyasūtras which give rather a brief account. They are the complete (almost exhaustive) works on the Saṃskāras. They elaborately explain the complete ritual and even ceremonies connected with the same. The Antyeṣṭi 'the funeral rite' is not described (or prescribed) by many Gṛhyasūtras, instead, this rite is separately dealt with in the Pitṛmedhasūtras. The reason for this exclusion of the funeral rite might be that the Antyeṣṭi was regarded as an inauspicious ceremony. The Prayoga- and Paddhati-texts, however, narrate the procedure of the funeral rite together with the other Saṃskāras.

The Saṃskāras are based mainly on the customs current in the society. Various Gṛhyasūtras and Prayoga-texts refer to such customs as can be classified broadly under three heads:

(i) *deśācāras* 'customs prevalent in a particular region',
(ii) *kūlācāras* 'customs peculiar to a relevant family',
(iii) *jātyācāras* 'customs current in a particular caste'.

This explains why the performance of a Saṃskāra shows variations in two distinct places.

Here, in this handbook of Saṃskāras, I have selected the procedure followed by the *Hiraṇyakeśigṛhyasūtra* [=HirGS] and the *Hiraṇyakeśibrahmakarmasamuccaya* [=HBKSam] (in the Pothī form) because the photographs which I have used in the illustration of the Saṃskāras, belong to the Natu family—the family which follows the Hiraṇyakeśi-sūtra of the Taittirīya Branch of Kṛṣṇa (i.e. black) Yajurveda. It is a well-known family in Pune city. They are Koṅkaṇastha (or, Chitpāvana) Brāhmaṇas by caste. The well-educated members of the family have contributed to the development and progress of the social as well as cultural activities in the city. They have got a family tradition maintained for more than 200 years in Pune. The first generation of the Natus in Pune can be traced back to the period earlier than the year 1800. Now, this family has seven generations residing in Pune. The religious Natu family performs various rituals, worships, *vratas* and ceremonies that are prescribed for the householders in the Hindu tradition. Ten out of sixteen Saṃskāras are performed in their family in the latest span of time, i.e. in the last twenty-five years. Hence many photographs were available to me and are of great use for me.

The method adopted in my book is to illustrate the procedure of the performance of a Saṃskāra with the help of the relevant photograph. Sometimes I have simply narrated the procedure and referred to the HBKSam, whereas, in some cases, I have quoted some significant Mantras when relevant to the context. The importance of such a work is valued in my opinion, in the field of sociology, as it covers the social and cultural aspect (or, phase) of today's Hindu religious society. The ceremonies and customs of every mode of their life depict their moral, psychological and spiritual attitude and approach towards their life and society as well. Keeping this in view, I have omitted all the Mantras or the Sanskrit portions referring to that relevant photographs in my illustrations. (Those, interested in the original Sanskrit text, may refer to the HirGS and the HBKSam).

The number of Saṃskāras differs in different traditions. The number varies from twelve to forty-eight. Among the various traditions, the Smṛtis, the Purāṇas and the Prayoga- and Paddhati-texts adopt sixteen Saṃskāras as main (or necessary) Saṃskāras and therefore, usually they elaborate sixteen Saṃskāras. Thus, these Saṃskāras, have received popularity as well as importance in Hindu tradition.

Also, there is a point of dispute regarding the order of the sixteen Saṃskāras. The Gṛhyasūtras mention the Saṃskāras in two different sequences. Many of them commence with the Vivāha and conclude with the Samāvartana. But the HirGS begins with the Upanayana, for it treats this as the foremost of the Saṃskāras. The HBKSam, differing from the HirGS, begins with the Garbhādhāna 'conception of a child in the womb of its mother' and ends with the Antyeṣṭi which is, obviously, the end of the life of an individual. The list of the sixteen Saṃskāras as dealt with by the HBKSam is as below:

NO.	NAME OF THE SAṂSKĀRA	AVAILABILITY
1	Garbhādhāna	O
2	Puṃsavana	O
3	Sīmantonnayana	O
4	Jātakarman	X
5	Nāmakaraṇa	O
6	Annaprāśana	O
7	Caula	O
8	Upanayana	O
9	Vedavratacatuṣṭaya (Prājāpatya)	X
10	Vedavratacatuṣṭaya (Saumya)	X
11	Vedavratacatuṣṭaya (Āgneya)	X
12	Vedavratacatuṣṭaya (Vaiśvadeva)	X
13	Godāna	X
14	Samāvartana	O
15	Vivāha	O
16	Antyeṣṭi	O

Besides the above-listed Saṃskāras, two ceremonies mentioned in the HBKSam are to be mentioned here. They are Niṣkramaṇa and Karṇavedha. They are added to or, introduced in the list of Saṃskāras by some Smṛtis and Purāṇas also.

Karṇavedha 'piercing of ears' is done before Nāmakaraṇa.

Niṣkramaṇa 'first outing' is referred to in the HBKSam [159B]. But, in modern times, instead of performing the rite according to the HBKSam, people customarily perform the Niṣkramaṇa. The first outing of the child, (of course) together with its mother, takes place any time after the fifth week of its birth. The mother and the child first go to the temple and later visit their relatives by whom they get blessed with presents and the lady of the relevant house pours some oil on the baby's head. In Pune, the practice is to go to Śītalādevī or Jogeśvarī temple as the place for the first outing.

All the Saṃskāras, with the exception only of Antyeṣṭi, invariably prescribe four preliminary rites and can be called the *pradhāna tantra* 'set pattern'. They are: Gaṇapatipūjana, Puṇyāhavācana, Mātṛkāpūjana and Nāndīśrāddha. As these preliminary rites are common to the fifteen Saṃskāras I have preferred to state them in the introductory portion in order to avoid the repetition. Though all the photographs used here for the illustration are from Vivāha, it is important to note that the other Saṃskāras also must include them. At the commencement of all the Saṃskāras, except the Antyeṣṭi, the performance of the four preliminaries is thus taken for granted (i.e. prescribed). In all these auspicious rites, the Yajamāna, who is first anointed together with his wife and son (or daughter), if the ceremony is meant for his son (or daughter in the marriage), has taken bath and has put a mark of *kuṅkuma* and then sits on a wooden plank, facing the east. His wife sits to his right. The son (or the daughter) also sits to the right of the mother. The Yajamāna begins with *ācamana* 'sipping water'. He sips water from the palm of his right hand three times and then performs *prāṇāyāma*, i.e. he holds in or restrains his breath. [see Fig. 15] Three of them bow down to the deities of the family and to the elderly persons of the household. Referring to the place and time, the Yajamāna declares what rite he is going to perform, for whom and for what purpose. He performs the four preliminaries as an inevitable (or compulsory) *aṅga* (subsidiary rite) to his rite.

Gaṇapatipūjana

It is a worship of Gaṇapati. Instead of placing an image/icon of Lord Gaṇapati, a betel-nut is placed on a handful of rice-grains and, the presence of the deity Gaṇapati is invoked on it with the recitation of the Mantra. [HBKSam: 84B, 2]

Thus, Lord Gaṇapati is invited along with his two wives, Ṛddhi and Siddhi, his *parivāra* 'retinue', his weapons, and his powers. He is worshipped with *ṣoḍaśopacāra* 'sixteenfold step of worship'. [cf. HBKSam: 84B, 4-7] In the prayer which comes at the end, the Yajamāna requests the Lord to remove the obstacles for the successful completion of the rite.

Puṇyāhavācana

This rite literally consists in invoking the Brāhmaṇas to declare the day to be auspicious for the rite which the Yajamāna is about to perform. To begin with, the Yajamāna, having touched and praised the ground, i.e. the earth, puts two small heaps of rice-grains on a wooden plank and places on them two pots full of water. He puts in them sandal-wood paste, flowers, Dūrvā grass and places five leaves (preferably of a mango tree) and two bowls filled with rice-grains on them. He, then, invokes Varuṇa's presence along with his retinue, weapons etc. in the pot, placed on the right side.

Fig. 1 The father (Yajamāna) touches two water-pots with both of his hands with the prayer. At the same time, his wife touches his right hand with her right hand and the son (or daughter) touches the mother's hand. (This signifies that these two also are participating in the action, performed by the Yajamāna.)

kalaśasya mukhe viṣṇuḥ kaṇṭhe rudraḥ samāśritaḥ/ mūle tatra sthito brahmā madhye mātṛgaṇāḥ smṛtāḥ// kukṣau tu sāgarāḥ sarve saptadvīpā vasundharā/ ṛgvedo 'tha yajurvedaḥ sāmavedo hy atharvaṇaḥ/ aṅgaiś ca sahitāḥ sarve kalaśaṃ tu samāśritāḥ/ atra gāyatrī sāvitrī śāntiḥ puṣṭikarī tathā/ āyāntu mama śāntyartham duritakṣayakārikāḥ/ sarve samudrāḥ saritas tīrthāni jaladā nadāḥ/ āyāntu mama śāntyartham duritakṣaya-kārakāḥ/ [HBKSam:122B, 10-13]

"Lord Viṣṇu occupies the mouth (i.e. opening part of the water-pot), while Rudra occupies the neck (i.e. the narrow part of the vessel). At the bottom (of it), Brahmā resides. The group of the *mātṛkās* are known as residing in the middle part. All the oceans and the earth, with its seven terrestial worlds, rest in the interior part of it. *Ṛg-*, *Yajus-*, *Sāma-* and *Atharvaveda*, together with all their auxilliary texts, have assembled in the water-pot. May here the hymn, composed in the *Gāyatrī* metre and addressed to the sun, may pacify evils (for me) and may it cause prosperity; may it come for effecting peace for me and may it avert evil (or, destroy calamities) for me. May all oceans, rivers, sacred streams, (rain-)clouds, flowing waters, which cause the destruction of evils, come for effecting peace for me."

He worships Varuṇa by offering the scent, flowers, sweet eatables, waving the lamp and, paying adoration, he recites the above-stated Mantras.

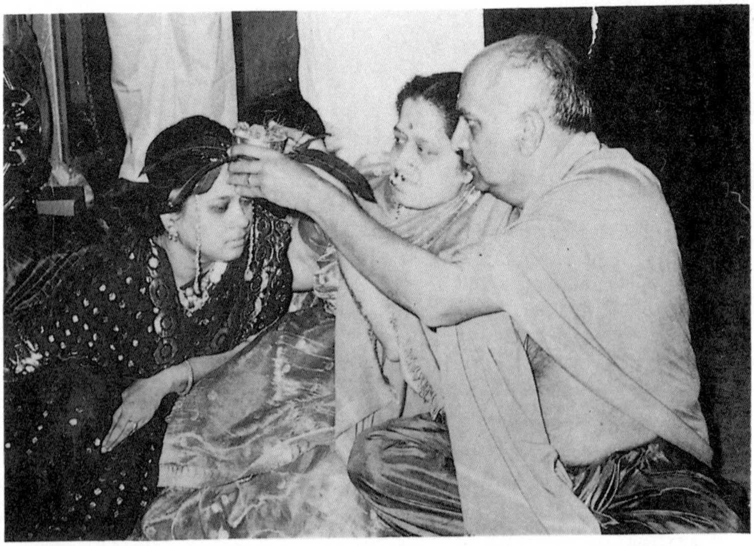

Fig. 2 The father of the bridegroom (or bride) touches the water-pot to the head of his son (or daughter).

The father holds the water-pot in his hands and touches it to the head of his son (or daughter) first and then to the head of his wife and (finally) of himself. Then he puts it on the place fixed for it. He repeats this procedure thrice.

The Yajamāna requests the Brāhmaṇas to declare the day to be auspicious for the rite. They respond by saying 'May it be auspicious.' Also, the Yajamāna requests the declaration of *svasti* and *ṛddhi*. The Brāhmaṇas respond accordingly. [HBKSam 124A, 9-124B, 6]

Fig. 3 An elderly lady in the house waves a lamp around the head of the three, viz. the son (or daughter), the wife and the Yajamāna in succession.

Then the Yajamāna holds the two pots in his hands and pours a continuous stream of the water from them. [HBKSam 125A, 1] The wife, now, sits to the left of the Yajamāna and the Brāhmaṇas sprinkle that water with the Dūrvā grass on the heads of all the three. At the end, the relatives give gifts to them.

Fig. 4

Mātṛkāpūjana

The Yajamāna places twenty-seven small heaps of rice-grains and invokes the presence of the mother goddesses, together with his family-deity, Gaṇapati, Vāstoṣpati etc. on them. The *mātṛkās*, 'mother-goddesses' comprise two groups, the group of sixteen *lokamātṛ(kā)*s, beginning with Gaurī, Padmā etc., and another group of seven *mātṛ(kā)*s beginning with Brāhmī, Māheśvarī etc. He, having established them on each of the heaps, worships them in sixteen steps. [HBKSam:126A, 2-6]

Nāndīśrāddha

This rite is performed on an occasion of Vṛddhi, i.e. an auspicious event in the house. The *nāndīmukha pitṛs* are worshipped by offering them *piṇḍas* 'the balls prepared of cooked rice'. The Yajamāna takes, in his hand, water, together with the Dūrvā grass, and some rice-grains and offers the same as the *pādya* 'water for cleansing the feet', to two Viśvadevas, viz. Satya and Vasu, and to a group of Pitṛs. This group comprises one's mother, paternal grandmother, paternal great grandmother; father, grandfather, great grandfather, and also generations of parents from the mother's side. Then the Yajamāna offers them a seat, worships them with the offering of sandal-wood paste, flowers etc. and solicits the blessings of the *nāndīmukha pitṛs* with the prayer that, being pleased with the worship, let the Pitṛs shower auspiciousness everywhere. He offers a feast and gifts to the Brāhmaṇas.

In the course of time, the Saṃskāras also, like all other rituals, have declined due to some factors which include the internal weakness of the performance and the external circumstances. As the new social and cultural forces worked on the society, some of the Saṃskāras have lost their original significance and became outdated. The individual, in modern times, is on occasions unable to perform the lengthy procedure of the performance and has, therefore, found some short-cuts, which would mean a serious attempt of reformation of the Saṃskāras, leaving out the lengthy ritual part and retaining only the kernel of the ceremony, considering the modern approach.

I have divided sixteen Saṃskāras into three groups; (1) those which are performed only rarely, (2) those which are performed briefly and (3) those which are important and always performed. Accordingly, they form the following group:

(1) Jātakarman and Vedavratacatuṣṭaya.
(2) Garbhādhāna, Puṃsavana, Sīmantonnayana, Nāmakaraṇa, Annaprāśana, Caula, Godāna, Samāvartana.
(3) Upanayana, Vivāha and Antyeṣṭi.

In the following sections, explanations of the sixteen Saṃskāras are organized in view the order of the HBKSam.

Sixteen Saṃskāras

(1) Garbhādhāna

It is a rite by the performance of which a man places his seed, i.e. semen in the womb of his wife. Garbhādhāna Saṃskāra is to be performed at the end of the three days of the first menstruation after marriage. On the fourth night, the husband asks the wife to accompany him, reciting nine specified Mantras. His successive actions, viz. embracing, kissing and cohabitation are accompanied by the recitation of various Mantras.

The medieval texts dicussing the Saṃskāras raise the question whether Garbhādhāna is the Garbha Saṃskāra, i.e. the Saṃskāra of the embryo or the Kṣetra Saṃskāra, i.e. the consecration of the wife. The HBKSam has decided that it is a Kṣetra Saṃskāra, as the Kṣetra once consecrated leads to purify every conception in future and hence the HBKSam prescribes Garbhādhāna rite to be performed only once, i.e. before the first cohabitation.

(2) Puṃsavana

After the conception is ascertained, the child in the womb is consecrated by the rite called Puṃsavana, the rite by virtue of which is assured a male child to be born. The proper time for this rite is the third month of the pregnancy. The day in the fortnight of the increasing moon, when the moon is on the male constellation, is regarded as favourable for the birth of a male child. The peculiarity of the HirGS lies in stating the venue for the performance of this rite and of the rite of Sīmantonnayana as well to be a round apartment.

The husband makes his wife to sit down facing the east. He puts a barley grain on her right hand. Then he puts two mustard seeds on both the sides of the barley grain and pours a drop of curds on those three grains and makes her eat the same without uttering any Mantra. After eating that mixture, when she sips water, the husband touches her abdomen, reciting the following Mantras:

abhi ṭvā ahaṃ daśabhir abhimṛśāmi daśamāsyāya sūtavai/ [HBKSam:153A, 1]

"I touch you with (my) ten (fingers) for a delivery in the tenth month."

Fig. 5a

Fig. 5b

Then he pounds the shoots or sprouts of a Nyagrodha (i.e. banyan) tree, mixes the juice with the ghee and inserts it into the right nostril of wife, whose head is resting on his laps.

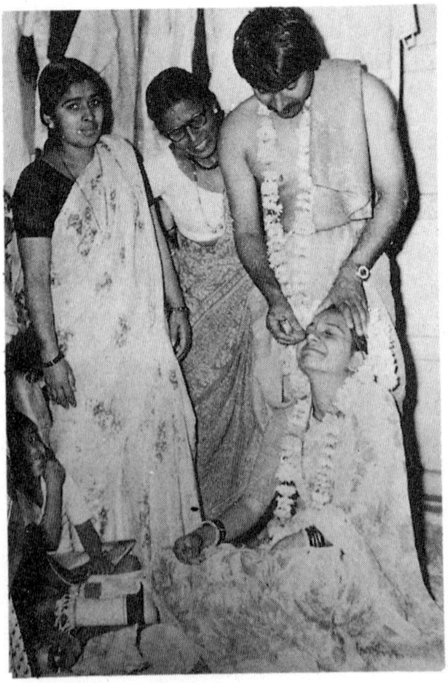

Fig. 6a

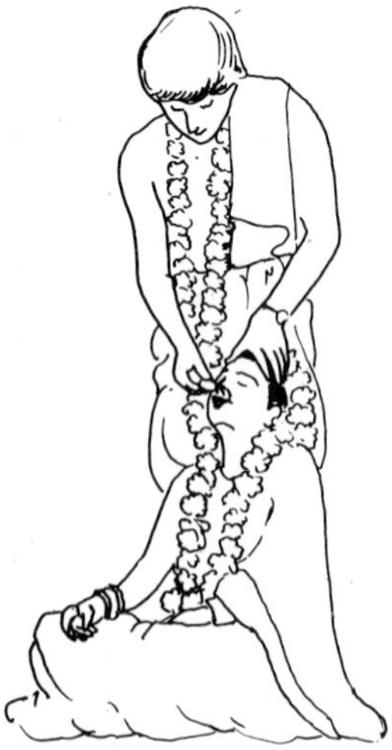

Fig. 6b

According to the local tradition, the followers of the Ṛgvedic Gṛhyasūtras use Dūrvā or Aśvagandhā 'bent grass' instead of the sprouts of a banyan tree.

The HirGS mentions the rite of Puṃsavana after the rite of Sīmantonnayana. But, the HBKSam records it before the Sīmantonnayana. The arrangement of the rites in the HBKSam appears more appropriate as it deals with the propriety of time-element considered in both the rites.

(3) Sīmantonnayana

The main feature of this rite is parting the hair of the pregnant wife by the husband. The proper time prescribed for this rite is the fourth month of pregnancy. The other details are similar to those of the Puṃsavana rite. The procedure of the rite is as follows:

Standing in front of the wife, who is facing the west, the husband parts her hair upwards, i.e. beginning from the front, with a porcupine's quill having three white spots, with a bunch of unripe fruits of Udumbara tree. The performance of the parting is accompanied by the three Vyāhṛtis and two Mantras. [HBKSam:153B, 8-12]

Fig. 7a

Fig. 7b

In modern times, these three Saṃskāras are rarely performed. Instead, in Maharashtra, some people perform a rite called *aṭhāṅguḷa* (in Marathi) in the eighth month of pregnancy. It retains the implications and the salient features of the above-mentioned three Saṃskāras, but, of course, in a shortcut manner.

Also, a social custom of keeping the pregnant woman in a cheerful mood is observed in the seventh month of her pregnancy. The ceremony is called *ḍohāḷa-jevaṇa* in Marathi. It is a feast to the pregnant woman. The food prepared is normally according to the wish and liking of the pregnant woman. Women gather together, often decorate her with garlands of flowers, sing songs for her and, thus, create a festive jubilant mood.

(4) Jātakarman

This rite is supposed to be performed before cutting the navel cord or, at least, immediately after the birth of the child. After the performance of four preliminaries, the father places an axe on a stone and puts some gold on the axe. Then he turns them upside down, thereby lies the stone on the top. He holds the child with his head eastwards above the stone and recites two Mantras [HBKSam:155A, 7-8], desiring that the son would be strong, sharp and worthy like the stone, the axe and the gold respectively. Then he takes the Aupāsanāgni, i.e. the regular Gṛhya fire away and brings Sūtikāgni, i.e. the fire inside the maternity room in which the child with its mother is confined. For the sake of protecting the child from evil spirits, he throws small rice-grains mixed with mustard seeds, into the Sūtikāgni, eleven times, with eleven Mantras. [HBKSam:155B, 1-8]

Then he washes the hands, touches the earth who is responsible for the safe delivery of the child and addresses her with gratitude. [HBKSam:155B, 9-10]

Then follows the rite of *medhājanana* 'production of intelligence'. The father holding the child, facing the east, feeds the clarified butter with a piece of gold, around which the Darbha grass is tied, along with three Mantras. [HBKSam:155B, 13-14]

Then he bathes the child with lukewarm water and puts him on the lap of his mother for breast-feeding. All these acts are accompanied by various Mantras. He keeps a pot full of water near the head of the child and the mother and praises the water to protect them while other people are sleeping.

This entire rite is not performed in modern times.[1]

(5) Nāmakaraṇa

Naming of the child (basically, this should refer to the son), according to the Hiraṇyakeśī tradition, should take place on the 12th day from the birth. The impurity caused by the birth of the son, for the parents, is regarded to be valid up to the 11th day. Hence, the proper time for naming would be the 12th day, i.e. after the parents being free from impurity. On the 12th day, the mother and the son take a bath. The father takes away the Sūtikāgni and, having replaced the Aupāsanāgni, he performs the four preliminaries and then the rites up to the Vyāhṛti oblations. He, then puts in the fire twelve/thirteen oblations with the Mantras. [HBKSam: 157B, 5-14]

The HBKSam, then records the social custom, prevalent in the Nāmakaraṇa Saṃskāra. The father takes a vessel of bronze, filled with rice-grains and thereon writes, with a gold pen, the words 'salutation to lord Gaṇapati' first and then four names of the son. The first name is given according to the family deity. Therefore, it is called *kuladevatānāma* with a view to securing special protection of the family deity. Then, he writes the second name, the *māsanāma*, based on the deity of the month in which the child is born. The third name is the *vyāvahārikanāma* or popular name which is meant for general use in the society. The last one is the *nākṣatranāma*, the name which is derived from the name of the constellation under which the child is born. The initial letter of the name is to be ascertained by deciding the *nakṣatra* under which the child is born, following the science of astrology.

Having written the four names on the rice-grains in the vessel, the father worships the *nāmadevatās* 'the deities presiding the names'. He leans towards his right where the mother sits with the son on her lap and declares the names in the right ear of the son. The priests assembled should say 'May the name be established.' Then he makes the son salute the priests and they bless him, addressing him by his four names.

The HirGS mentions only three names, the first *vyāvahārika*, the second *nākṣatra* and the third *somayājin* (performer of Soma sacrifice). Following the Gṛhyasūtra, the HBKSam mentions this tra-

1. Apteji, the officiating priest of the Natus, orally reported that he has never performed this rite in last fifty years.

dition also. Also, corresponding the text of the Gṛhyasūtra, it adds that the *nākṣatra* name should be secret and it is known only to the parents. The son comes to know it on the occasion of the Upanayana.

*[The Nāmakaraṇa Saṃskāra was performed in the case of Girīśa, son of the Natus and the Baṭu on the occasion of Upanayana seen below The four names given at that time are as follows:

śrīyogeśvarībhakta as the *kuladevatānāma* and *vaikuṇṭha* as the *māsanāma*; as he was born on the 11th day of the black fortnight of the month of Caitra. His *vyāvahārika* name is Girīśa and the *nākṣatra* name is *dhāniṣṭheya* as the constellation under which he is born is *dhaniṣṭhā*. The four letters, viz. gā gī, gū and ge are presided over by the constellation *dhaniṣṭhā* [cf. HBKSam:158B, 14] and hence the *vyāvahārika* name chosen was Girīśa, beginning with the letter *gi*.]

In modern times, the naming ceremony takes place on the 12th day after the birth of the baby, or according to convenience. The procedure prescribed in the Gṛhyasūtras is not performed. But a ceremony of social importance takes place. Women assemble and two elderly women in the household of the father and the mother respectively place the child in the cradle and the mother(or paternal aunty) whispers the name (only the popular one) in the ear of the baby.

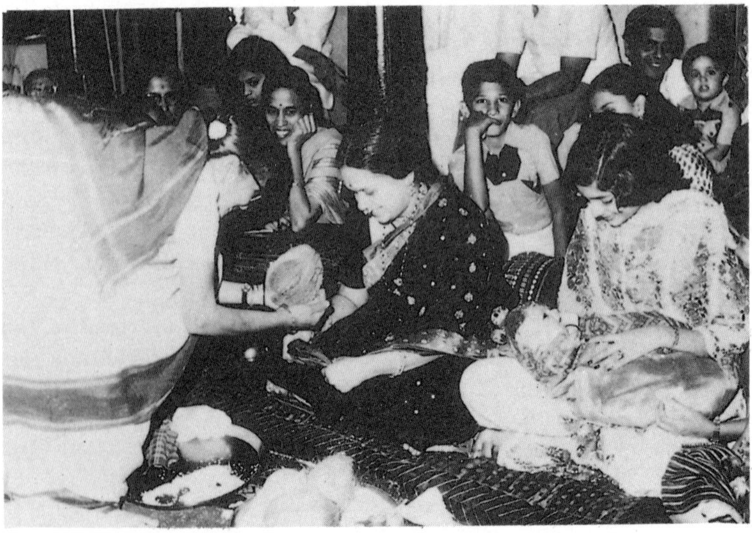

Fig. 8

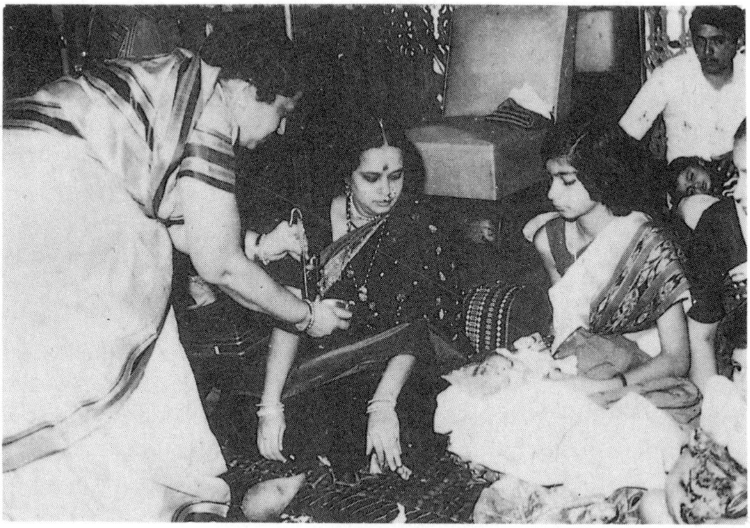

Fig. 9

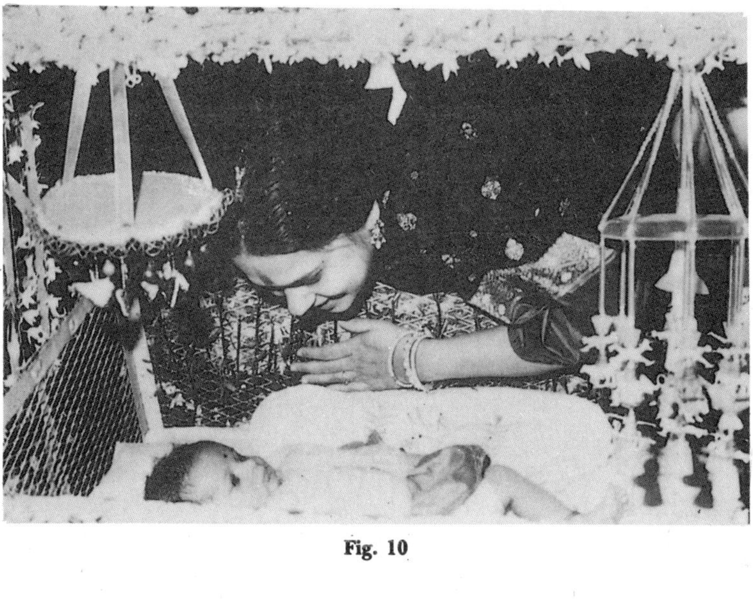

Fig. 10

(6) Annaprāśana

The significance of the rite of Annaprāśana is to make the child eat the cooked or rather solid food for the first time. The proper time for this Saṃskāra prescribed by the HirGS is the sixth month from the birth of the child. The HBKSam alternatively suggests the eighth month from the birth. This Saṃskāra should be performed after the appearance or growth of at least one or two teeth. The auspicious time for this Saṃskāra is the first fortnight of the month under an auspicious constellation.

The HBKSam states that, among these sixteen Saṃskāras, Annaprāśana, Caula and Godāna do not require *vaiśeṣika-homa* 'special sacrifice'. But all the same, it prescribes an *upahoma* 'a supplementary sacrifice' and the performance up to the *vyāhṛti* oblations 'oblation with the utterance of the names of seven worlds (viz. *bhūḥ, bhuvaḥ* and *svaḥ*)'. This *homa* is preceded by the four preliminary rites, viz. Gaṇapatipūjana etc., like all other Saṃskāras.

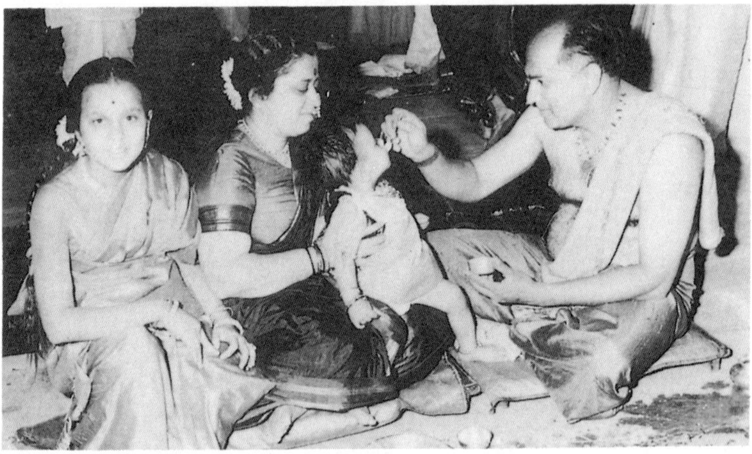

Fig. 11

The HBKSam describes the father giving the child, who is sitting to his right on the lap of his mother and facing him, the threefold food (the mixture of curds, honey and ghee) to eat, with the recitation of the Mantras:

bhūs tvayi dadhāmi/ bhuvas tvayi dadhāmi/ suvas tvayi dadhāmi/ [HBKSam:160B, 9]

"Bhuḥ I lay into thee! Bhuvaḥ, I lay into thee! Suvaḥ, I lay into thee!" [SBE:216]

> *apāṃ tvā oṣadhīnām rasaṃ prāśayāmi śivās te āpa oṣadhayaḥ santv anamīvās te āpa oṣadhayo bhavantu/* [HBKSam:160B, 9-10]
> "I give thee to eat the essence of water and of the plants. May water and plants be kind towards thee. May water and plants do no harm to thee." [SBE:216]

The HBKSam mentions that the Annaprāśana of the female child is to be performed with the same procedure, but without the Mantras.

Also, the HBKSam states one more interesting feature. After the feeding is over, various things, such as scriptures, weapons, tools and utensils required in various arts and crafts should be kept in front of the child. Which of them the child handles first would be deemed as the profession of his livelihood.

In the modern days, this rite is performed in the case of every child, but with a vast difference. Of course, the performance of a *homa* etc. are omitted and the feeding of the child is done not by the father but by the maternal uncle without the accompanying Mantras. The maternal uncle brings a plate, a bowl and a wooden seat for the child and feeds him with something made of gold (for instance, a gold ring) dipped in the sweet *khīra* (in Marathi [=*kṣīra* in Sanskrit]) which is made of milk, sugar and *śevai* (a noodle-like stuff in Marathi).

Fig. 12

(7) Caula

The Caula Saṃskāra is the first tonsure or cutting of the hair on the child's head. According to the HirGS, the Caula is to be performed in the third year from the birth. But the HBKSam gives the option of five years also. But, in case it is not performed in its proper time, the Caula should be necessarily performed before the Upanayana—a day before the Upanayana or at least on the day of the Upanayana, i.e. before initiation.

Initially, a *homa* is performed and the oblations are given in the Aupāsanāgni, called *sabhya.* The boy sits down to the right of his parents, facing the east. The father sits in front of the fire and the mother or a Brahmacārin (holding a lump of a bull's dung) to the north of the fire; for she (or the Brahmacārin) is supposed to gather the hair cut by the father. The father pours hot water in the cold water and moistens therewith the hair near the right ear of the son, reciting the Mantra:

> *āpa undantu jīvase dīrghāyutvāya varcase/*
> "May the waters moisten thee for life, for long life and for lustre."

Then reciting the following Mantra, he puts herb, with its points upwards into the hair.

> *oṣadhe trāyasvainam/*
> "O herb, protect him!"

He touches both the hair and the herb with the razor, reciting the Mantra:

> *svadhite mainaṃ hiṃsīḥ/*
> "O axe, do not harm him!"

Then, reciting the Mantra below, he shaves in one direction.

> *devaśrūr etāni pravape/*
> "O (axe) heard by the gods, I shave that (hair)."

The same procedure is followed for shaving in the other three directions. Only the Mantras for the act of shaving vary. [HBKSam:162A,11-162B, 2]

Then, the barber shaves the hair cleanly and arranges the locks according to the local custom, or according to the family tradition. A close relative of the child collects the cut-off hair and buries the same in a cow-stable, or near an Udumbara tree, or in a clump of Darbha grass, reciting the Mantra. [HBKSam:162B, 7-8] The father gives food and gifts to the Brāhmaṇas and boiled rice, with clarified butter on it, to the barber.

In the modern days, the Caula, as it is stated previously, is performed normally on the same day as of the Upanayana. But, in the case of a son, the first cutting of his hair takes place at the time of the Annaprāśana, i.e. in the sixth or eighth month from the birth. In Marathi, it is called *jāvaḷa.* The father or maternal uncle takes the child on his lap and the barber cuts the hair. The paternal aunty collects the cut-off hair and, is then honoured by her brother with a gift (the gift is supposed to be gold equal to the weight of the cut-off hair she collected.)

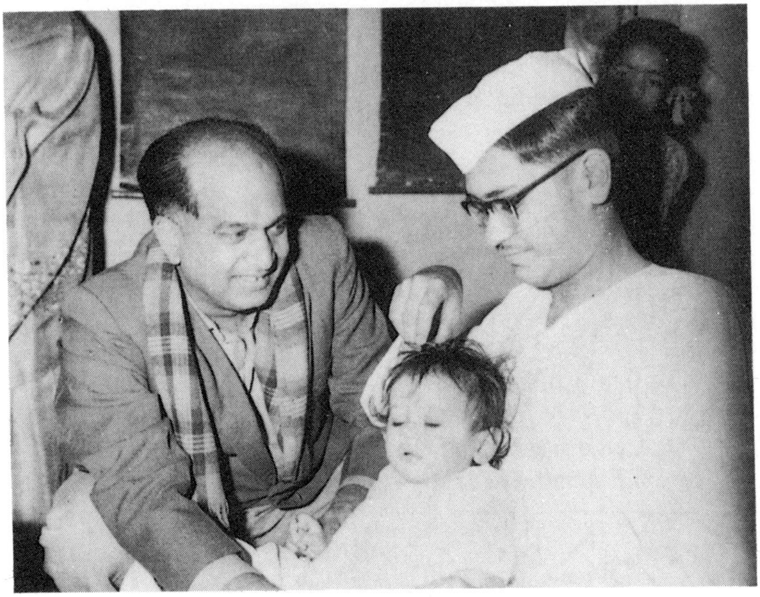

Fig. 13

(8) Upanayana

TITLES	FIG NOS.	DIVISIONS
i. *Ghāṇā*	14/15	xxxx
ii. Four Preliminary Rites	—	xxx
iii. *Maṇḍapadevatāpratiṣṭhā*	16/17	xxx
iv. *Grahayajña*	—	xxx
v. *Mātṛbhojana*	18	xxx
vi. Offering Oblations	19	xx
vii. *Aśmārohaṇa*	20/21/22	xx
viii. *Bohole*	23	xxx
ix. Recitation of Benedictory Verses (*Maṅgalāṣṭaka*)	24	xxx
x. Removal of a Parting-cloth	25	xxx
xi. Waving the Lamp around the Baṭu's Face	26	xxx
xii. Holding his Hand by Father	27	xx
xiii. *Agniparicaryā*	28/29/30	xx
xiv. *Daṇḍagrahaṇa*	31	xx
xv. *Bhikṣā*	32	xx
xvi. *Gāyatrī Upadeśa*	33	xx
xvii. *Baṭupūjana*	34	xxxx
xviii. Procession	35/36	xxxx
xix. Welcoming the Baṭu and his Mother	37	xxxx
xx. *Maṇḍapadevatotthāpana*	—	xxx
xxi. *Satyanārāyaṇa Pūjā*	38/39	xxxx

xx Vedic Ritual
xxx Post-Vedic Addition in Medieval Period
[xxxx: This is not noticeable in xx nor xxx but is seen in actual performance in Maharashtra. Therefore, I call it as expression of certain customs which prevail possibly during the last two centuries. About this date, we cannot be certain. Also, I have made an observation only on what I actually noticed in Pune. Possibly, some of these practices might be noticed in similar ritual in other parts of India also. Therefore, I do not call them purely local Maharashtrian customs.]

(i) *Ghāṇā*

This is grinding of the *māṣas* 'beans', done by the ladies of the family before the performance of Upanayana or Vivāha. This is a local tradition. Before industrialization, grinding was done at home with the help of two wheels made up of stone. That traditional action is performed as the symbol of the beginning of the preparations for the ceremony.

Fig. 14

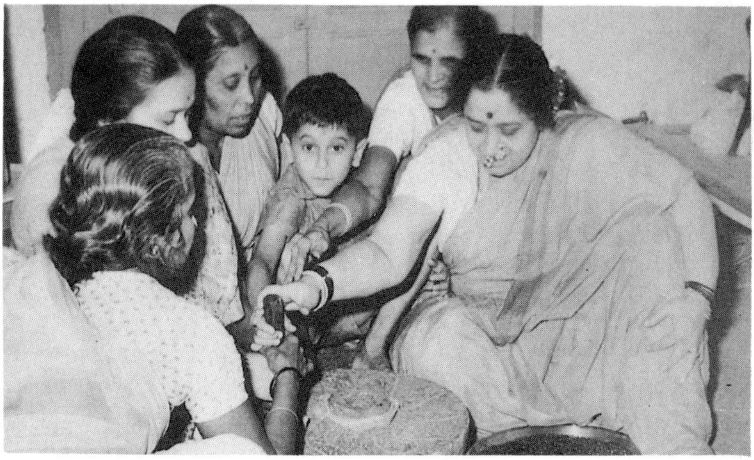

Fig. 15

(ii) Four Preliminary Rites, see Introduction (pp.94-99)

(iii) *Maṇḍapadevatāpratiṣṭhā*

After the rite of *Puṇyāhavācana* is over, the Yajamāna performs a rite called *Maṇḍapadevatāpratiṣṭhā*. This rite is called *devadevaka* in Marathi. The Yajamāna takes six leaves of a mango tree and encircles them sixteen times with a thread, and then he takes a shallow basket or a winnowing pan of bamboo (*sūpa* in Marathi and *śūrpa* in Sanskrit), with a piece of cloth and rice-grains spread on it, and places six leaves together with a coconut to the left. He puts twenty-seven batel-nuts to the right and an earthen pot in the middle. The pot is called *avighna-pa-kalaśa* 'a picture which protects (towards completion of the rite) without any difficulty or hindrance'. It is filled with rice-grains, a betel-nut and a piece of termeric and is covered with a shallow earthen dish. A thread is tied around it.

Fig. 16a

Fig. 16b

The Yajamāna invites the presence of the deities, called Nandinī, Nalinī, Maitrā, Umā, Paśuvardhinī, Śastragarbhabhagavatī in the leaves and of Gaṇapati in the *kalaśa* respectively by offering rice-grains to them. The Yajamāna then offers them a seat, water for cleansing the feet, *arghya* and *acamanīya* 'water of drinking'.

Fig. 17a

Fig. 17b

The Yajamāna then lifts the *kalaśa* with the deities installed in them and places the same in another dish. He anoints the deities with scented oil and showers lukewarm water on them. Then he places them again in their respective positions and worships by various modes of worship, viz. offering them clothing, sandal-wood paste, rice-grains, flowers, *dhūpa*, waving a lamp, offering food, fruits and betel-leaves etc. He himself lifts the basket, gives the *avighnapakalaśa* to his wife and both of them place them in the house where they daily worship their family-deity. These *maṇḍapadevatās* are to be worshipped until the ceremony which is undertaken is over.

(iv) *Grahayajña*

Grahayajña is a sacrifice performed for seeking the favour of the planets. It is performed together with the preliminary rites of the Upanayana as well as of the Vivāha. For details, see Vivāha, *Grahayajña*. (pp.136-138)

(v) *Mātṛbhojana*

Mātṛbhojana is the most popular custom in the Upanayana ceremony and it takes place in the morning before the actual procedure of the Upanayana rite starts. It is a ceremonial meal for the Baṭu (the boy) to be initiated. He takes his meals together with his mother in the same plate for the last time. (Later, he is not supposed to do so as stated below.) On this occasion, eight Brahmacārins 'initiated Baṭus', his friends and other children in the household accompany him while eating the meal. This ceremony reflects the close association of the Baṭu with his mother. In the childhood, mother very affectionately feeds the child. Also, very often, he takes meals together with her in her plate. But, now after the Upanayana, the Baṭu will have to lead a disciplined life and various restrictions would not allow him to take food with his mother or, any elderly lady, like an aunt (for instance). Hence, mother feeds the Baṭu with her hand. The elderly women in the household also feed him. After this feast is over, the head of the Baṭu is shaved and then he takes a bath, wears the clothes, which are not washed before.

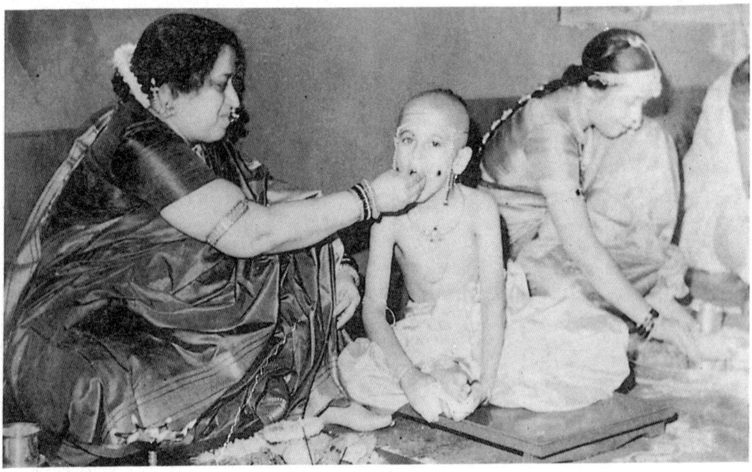

Fig. 18

The father kindles a new worldly fire, or fetches fire from *agnyāgāra.* He puts wood into it. He strews Darbha grass pointing westwards.

All the utensils and other material, which are necessary for a *homa,* are collected together around the fire. Also, the essential things for the Baṭu (for example, a *yajñopavīta, mekhalā, daṇḍa, ajina, bhikṣāpātra*) are brought together. Then the Baṭu puts on a *kaṭisūtra*. He sips water and wears the *yajñopavīta*, reciting the Mantra. [HBKSam:173A, 9-10]

(vi) Offering Oblations

The Baṭu then sits on the right side of the father, facing the fire. The father offers oblations with Mantras. [HBKSam:173B, 2-4]

Fig. 19

(vii) *Aśmārohaṇa* Fig. 20b

The father brings the Baṭu to the northern side where a stone is placed and makes him stand on it placing his right foot first. [HBKSam:173B, 6] The Baṭu takes off his old garment and the father makes him wear a new one.

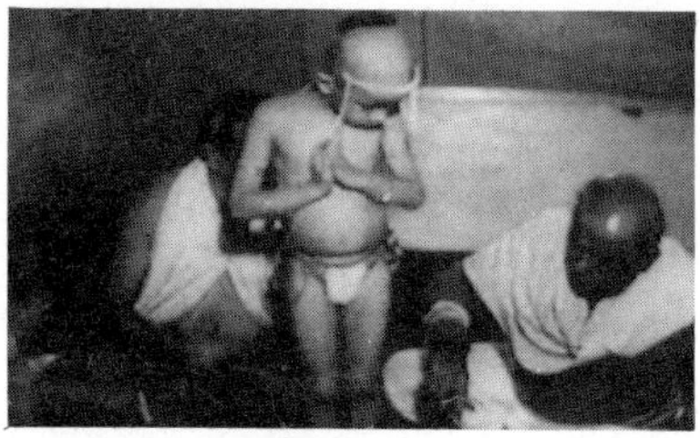

Fig. 20a

Fig. 20b

The father winds the gridle of Muñja grass around his waste thrice from left to right covering his navel. [HBKSam:173B, 11-12] Then he makes him put on the skin of an antelope as the upper garment. The father now assigns the Baṭu to the charge of the gods, reciting various Mantras. He askes the Baṭu to sit to the west of the fire, facing the north and to eat the remnants of the sacrificial food, or the clarified butter mixed with curds. After then, the Baṭu sips water and touches the father.

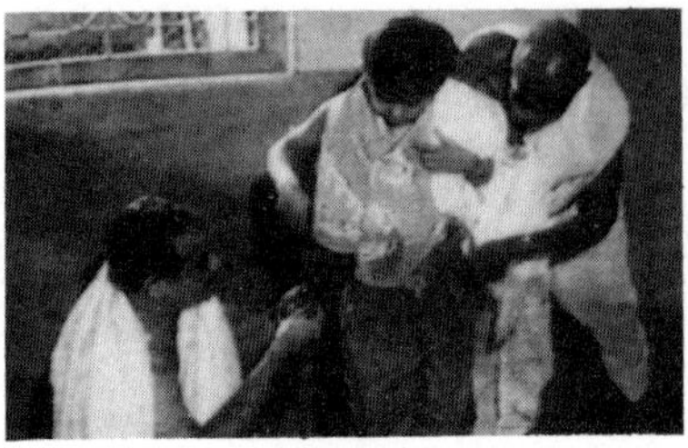

Fig. 21a

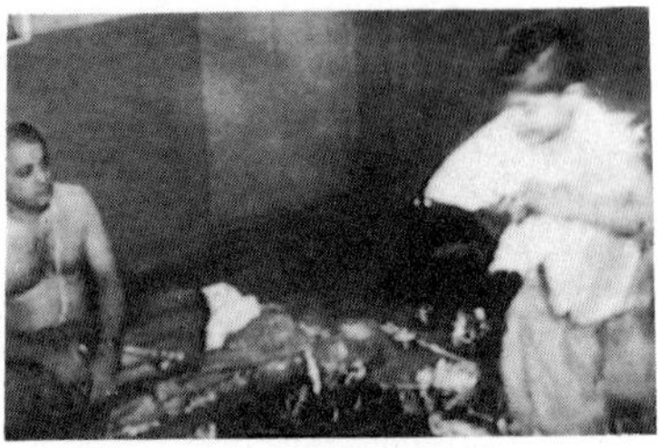

Fig. 22a

Fig. 21b

Fig. 22b

While the Baṭu walks around the fire, keeping his right side turned towards it, the father recites some prescribed verses. [HBKSam: 174A, 11]

The Baṭu requests the father, who is supposed to be his teacher, that he has come there for studies and, therefore, he wants to be initiated. The father asks him his name and, in reply, the Baṭu tells his popular name and the *nākṣatra* name as well.

(viii) *Bohole*

The father and the Baṭu purify themselves by sprinkling water on themselves with the blades of Kuśa grass. After this sprinkling, they wait for the *muhūrta*, i.e. the auspicious time, of the Upanayana. This is a picture of Bohole (in Marathi meaning 'raised platform'). It is the appointed place for the ceremony on which the Upanayana rite would take place.

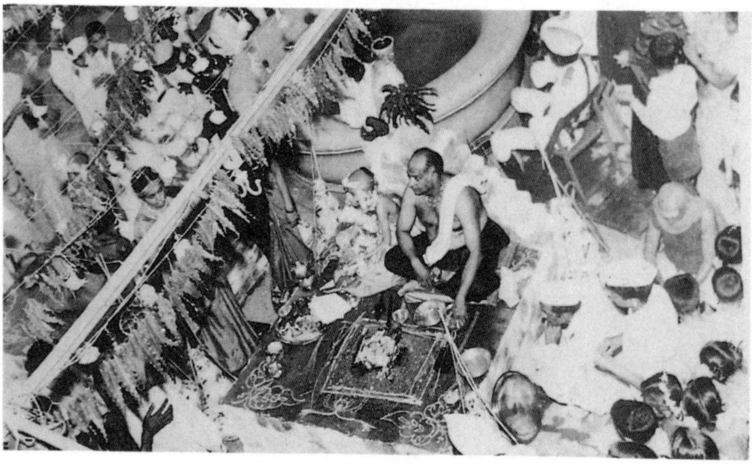

Fig. 23

(ix) Recitation of Benedictory Verses

Then a secular custom of reciting eight auspicious, benedictory verses, is observed. All the relatives and the friends, who have gathered to attend the ceremony, assemble around the Baṭu who is standing, facing his father, and the two priests who stand holding a piece of cloth between the Baṭu and the father. Two sisters stand behind the Baṭu, one holding a lamp in her hand and the other holding a pot full of water, covered with mango-leaves and a coconut. The priests recite eight verses, expressive of the blessings to the Baṭu. The invitees throw (i.e. sprinkle, as though) rice-grains on the Baṭu, after the completion of each verse. This recitation is completed at the *muhūrta* settled for the Upanayana.

Fig. 24

(x) Removal of the Parting-cloth

Exactly at the time of the *muhūrta,* the piece of cloth which was held between the father and the Baṭu is removed away and the Baṭu goes near his father, bows down to him and, as a token of gratitude, offers a coconut-fruit to him. The father, looking at him, makes him sit in front of him, or on his lap.

Fig. 25

(xi) Waving the Lamp around the Baṭu's Face

One of the two sisters, the one with a lamp in the hand, proceeds and waves the lamp around the faces of the father and the son.

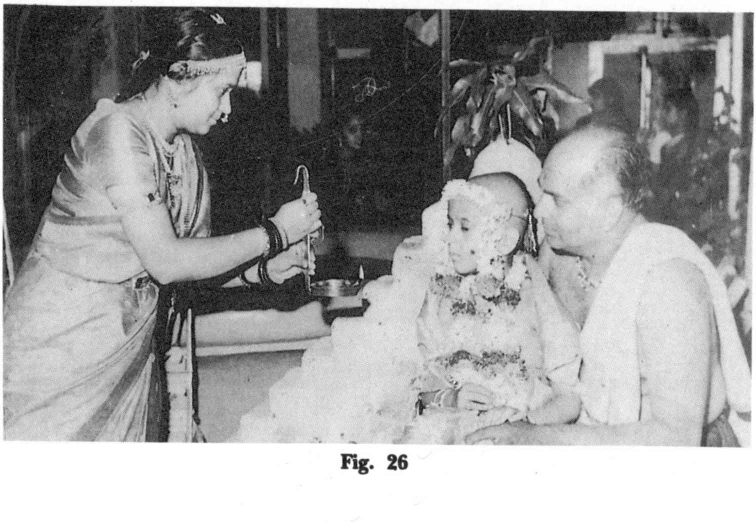

Fig. 26

Then the father touches the right shoulder of the Baṭu with his right hand, his left shoulder with his left hand, and, then with his right hand, he touches the heart of the Baṭu and makes him sit near him. The father seizes his right hand which is turned upwards together with the thumb with his right hand. Afterwards, the father gradually moves his hand over the Baṭu's right shoulder and touches his heart. [HBKSam:175A, 11] This act signifies their hearts as well as minds are well-united. Such union is necessary or beneficial for initiation.

(xii) Holding his Hand by Father

Then the father touches the Baṭu's navel. The father holds his right hand with reciting the verses. [HBKSam:175B, 4-6] Then he recites two Mantras, both in each of the Baṭu's ears and, bringing his face near, the father recites another Mantra. Then he assigns the Baṭu to charge of the gods.

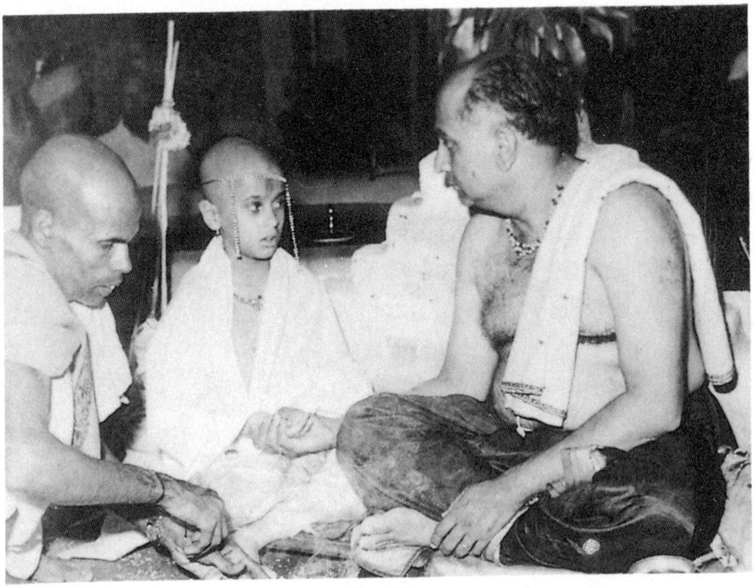

Fig. 27

(xiii) *Agniparicaryā*

The father makes the Baṭu to offer pieces of Palāśa wood into the fire. He makes seven oblations of Palāśa leaves dipped in the ghee.

Fig. 28

agnaye samidham āhārṣam bṛhate jātavedase/ yathā tvam agne samidhā samidhyasa evam mām medhayā prajñayā prajayā paśubhir brahmavarcasenānnādyena samedhayā svāhā/ [HBKSam:176A, 6-7]

"To Agni I have brought a piece of wood, to the great Jātavedas....." [SBE:155]

Fig. 29

In the first offering, he offers one *samidh* (fuel/sacrificial stick) for the sacred fire, in the second, two and, in the last, the remaining four; each time the same Mantra being recited.
Then the father completes the ritual.

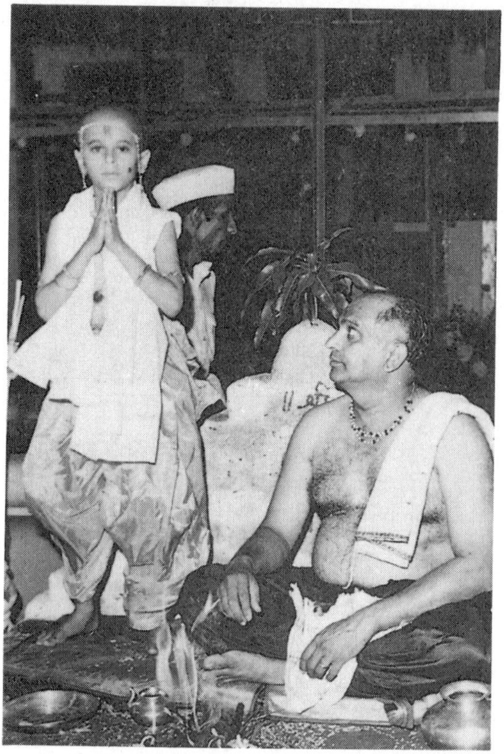

Fig. 30

The Baṭu takes the vows that are to be kept in the first order of life (viz. Brahmacarya). The father expounds the vows or modes of behaviour prescribed for a Brahmacārin. The Baṭu, aiming at the prescribed duties of the first order of life, prays—

> *agne vratapate vrataṃ cariṣyāmi tac chakeyaṃ tan me rādhyatām/*
> *vāyo vratapate vrataṃ cariṣyāmi tac chakeyaṃ tan me rādhyatām/*
> *āditya vratapate vrataṃ cariṣyāmi tac chakeyaṃ tan me rādhyatām/*
> *vratānāṃ vratapate vrataṃ cariṣyāmi tac chakeyaṃ tan me rādhyatām* / [HBKSam:176A, 12-13]
>
> "O Agni, the lord of vows, I shall (hereafter) observe the vow. May I be able to do it. May that be complete for me.

"O Vāyu, the lord of vows, I shall (hereafter) observe the vow. May I be able to do it. May that be complete for me.
"O Āditya, the lord of vows, I shall (hereafter) observe the vow. May I be able to do it. May that be complete for me.
"O lord of vows, I shall (hereafter) observe the vow. May I be able to do it. May that be complete for me."[cf. SBE:156]

These vows are to be observed till the time of the Samāvartana. The Baṭu gives a gift to the father, who is regarded as the teacher. The father makes him stand and assigns him to the charge of the sun. The Baṭu (then) worships the sun.

(xiv) *Daṇḍagrahaṇa*

The father hands over to the Baṭu the stuff with the following Mantra:

agniṣ ṭa āyuḥ pratarāṃ kṛṇotv agniṣ ṭe puṣṭiṃ pratarāṃ dadhātvindro marudbhir iha te dadhātu ādityas te vasubhir ā dadhātu/ [HBKSam:176B, 6]

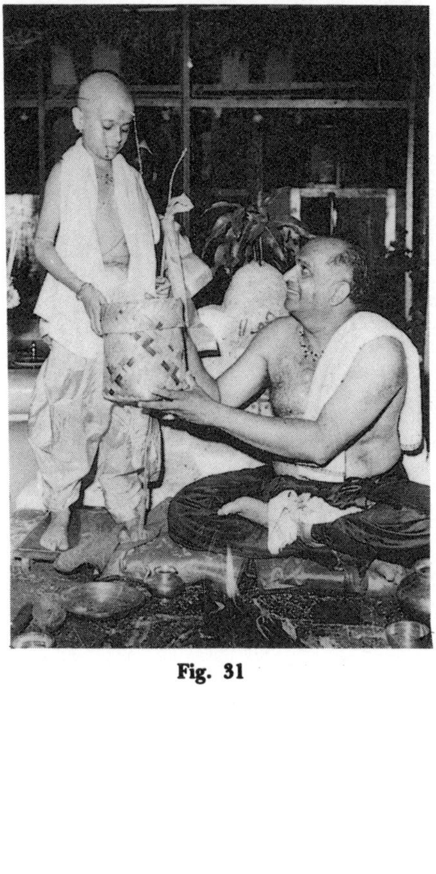

Fig. 31

"May Agni further give thee life. May Agni further grant thee bliss. May Indra with the Maruts here give (that) to thee; may the sun with the Vasus give (it) to thee." [SBE:157]

And then silently he gives him a bowl for collecting the alms and asks him:

bhikṣācaryaṃ cara [HBKSam:176B, 7]

"Go out for alms."[SBE:157]

(xv) *Bhikṣā* 'begging for food'

The Baṭu accepts the orders of the father and, accordingly, he first goes to his mother for alms and then to the other women, who are affectionate to him like his mother, (and also to others) and says to each one of them,

Oṃ bhavati bhikṣāṃ dehi/

Or, *Oṃ bhavān bhikṣāṃ dadātu/* [HBKSam:176B, 8]

"O honourable lady/sir, give me some food."

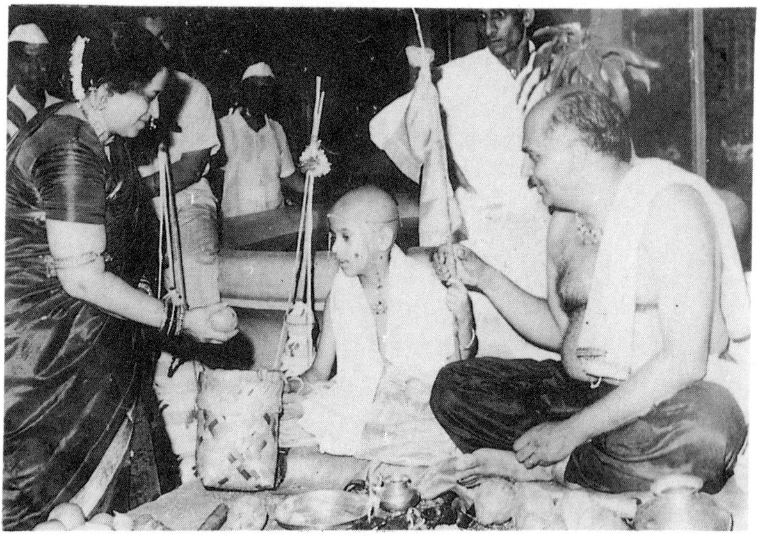

Fig. 32

Then she/he gives him some eatable as alms. The Baṭu returns to his father and gives unto him the alms he could get. The father accepts the same. The father sits, facing the east, for the initiation of the Gāyatrī Mantra. The Baṭu bows down to the sun and touches the right foot of the father and requests him to initiate him. [HBKSam:177A, 2-5]

(xvi) *Gāyatrī Upadeśa*

Then the father gives the initiation of the Gāyatrī Mantra, which is the first lesson of the teacher (=father).

(Gāyatrī Mantra= *Ṛgveda* 3.62.10)

Oṃ bhūs tat savitur vareṇyaṃ (That adorable splendour) / *bhuvo bhargo devasya dhīmahi* (of the divine Savitṛ may we obtain) / *suvar dhiyo yo naḥ pracodayāt* (who should rouse our prayers) / / *Oṃ bhūr bhuvas tat savitur vareṇyaṃ bhargo devasya dhīmahi/ suvar dhiyo yo naḥ pracodayāt// Oṃ bhūr bhuvaḥ suvaḥ/ tat savitur vareṇyaṃ bhargo devasya dhīmahi/ dhiyo yo naḥ pracodayāt//* [HBKSam:177A, 9-11] [SBE:155]

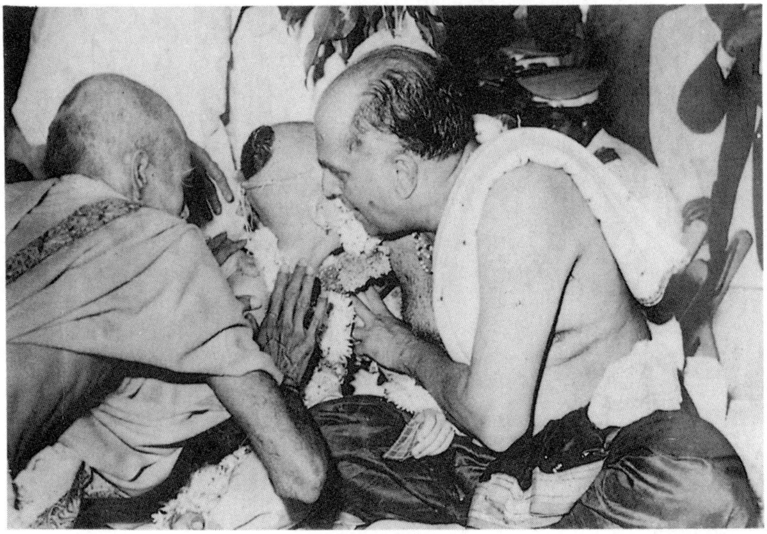

Fig. 33

According to the followers of the Taittirīya branch, the study of all the Vedas begins with the initiation of the Gāyatrī Mantra.

(xvii) *Baṭu-pūjana*

The young Brahmacārin is looked upon as the *baṭumūrti* of Vāmana, one of the incarnations of Lord Viṣṇu. Thus, he is highly esteemed. The old lady of the house worships the Baṭu and, with devotion, drinks the *tīrtha* 'water with which she washed his feet that turned holy'.

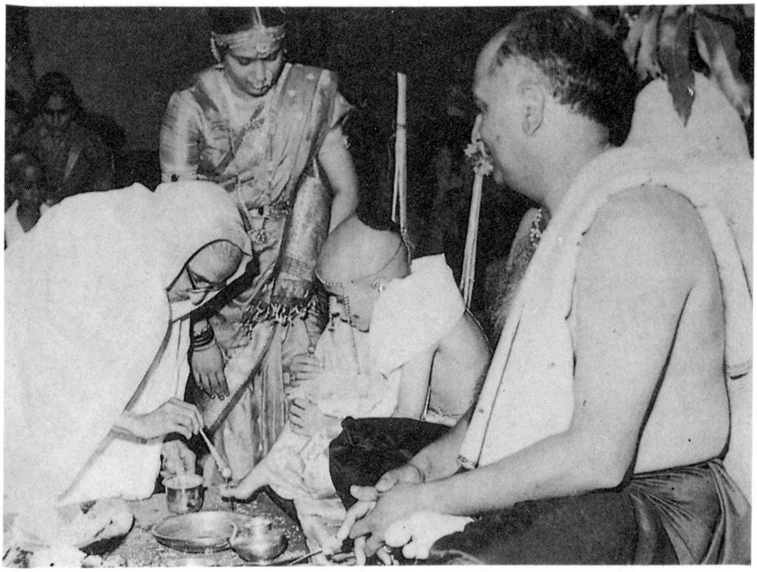

Fig. 34

The *lokācāra* has modified the ritual of begging for alms and gave rise to the custom of *Bhikṣāvaḷa* (in Marathi) as it is called in Maharashtra. It means taking the Baṭu around the town in a procession. A well-dressed Baṭu sits in a vehicle, decorated with flowers. He is headed by a group of people playing the band (or musical instruments) and is followed by the relatives.

(xviii) Procession

(In Pune) the procession starts from the place of the Upanayana. It leads to the Kasabā Gaṇapati and Jogeśvarī—the two *grāmadevatās* of Pune. The Baṭu, accompanied by his relatives, visits these two temples and, after worshipping the deities, seeks the blessings of the two gods.

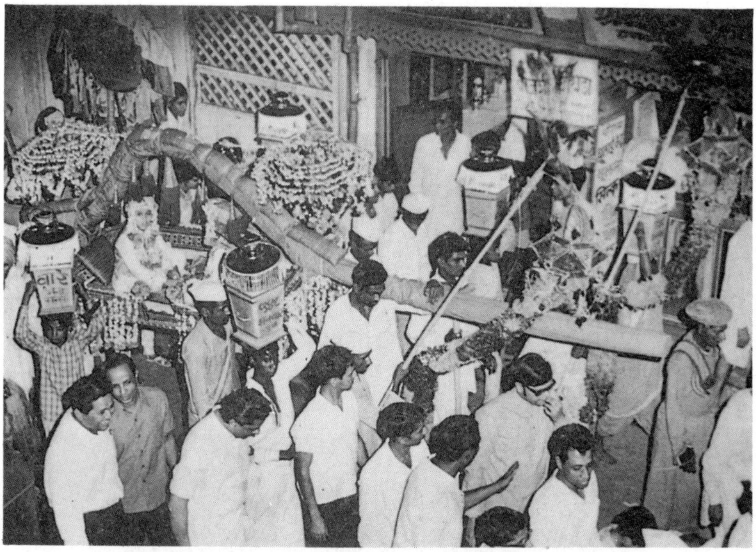

Fig. 35

Fig. 36

The procession in front of the *Śaniwāra Wāḍā*. The *Pālakhī* 'palanquin' by which the Baṭu went to the temples is a vehicle which is carried away by men. It is a sign of honour which was given to the *Saradāras* by the Peshwas.

(xix) Welcoming the Baṭu and his Mother

When the procession returned, an elderly lady of the family welcomed the Baṭu and his mother by waving the lamp around his face.

After returning home, the Baṭu, holding the stuff in his left hand and the bowl in the right hand, begs his mother for alms. The mother puts some eatable into the bowl. She is followed by other women also.

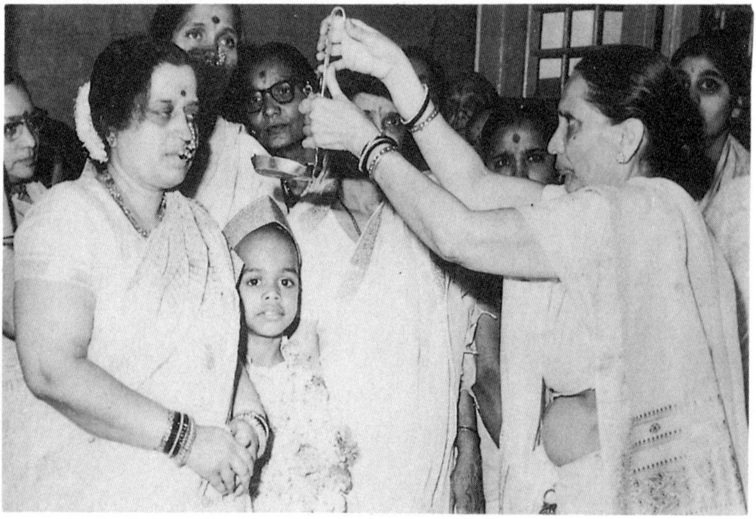

Fig. 37

(xx) *Maṇḍapadevatotthāpana*

Thereafter, the Yajamāna and his wife lift the *śurpa* and the *avighnapa-kalaśa* respectively from the place where they were placed before the Upanayana ceremony and the concluding rite starts. At the commencement, the Yajamāna performs the *Puṇyāhavācana*. Then he worships the deities in sixteen steps (*Ṣoḍaśopacāra pūjā*) and bids them good-bye. [HBKSam:178B, 10]

Among the sixteen Saṃskāras, these rites called *Maṇḍapadevatāpratiṣṭhā*, *Grahayajña* and *Maṇḍapadevatotthāpana*, are performed only in two Saṃskāras, viz. Upanayana and Vivāha. Similar is the case with the *Satyanārāyaṇa Pūjā*. So, these rites, except the *Grahayajña*, are elaborately narrated here and in the description of Vivāha, they are just referred to.

(xxi) *Satyanārāyaṇa Pūjā*

This Pūjā is performed on every auspicious occasion, invariably after the Upanayana or Vivāha. The deity to be worshipped is Viṣṇu. At the beginning, the worship of the Gaṇapati is performed. It is followed by the worship of eight *lokapālas* and nine *grahas* 'planets'. Then Lord Viṣṇu is worshipped in the manner of *ṣoḍaśopacāra*. It is followed by the offering of 1,000 leaves of Tulasī plant accompanied by the utterance of *viṣṇusahasranāma* (i.e. of 1,000 names of Lord Viṣṇu). *Dhūpa*, a lamp (i.e. *dīpa*), and the offering of *śirā* (a preparation of wheat, ghee, sugar and milk) is offered to him. Then, a certain *kathā* 'story' is narrated as the *phalaśruti* 'describing the result of the performance'. *Uttarapūjā* 'the final or concluding worship' is then performed. It consists in worship in *pañcopacāra*, viz. offering *gandha* 'sandal-wood paste', *puṣpa* 'flower', *dhūpa*, *dīpa* 'lamp', and *naivedya* 'an offering'. Then the *mahānaivedya* 'the offering of the meals' is offered. The *pūjā* concludes with the *ārātrika* (*āratī* in Marathi), salutation and offering of flowers with the recitation of Mantras.

Fig. 38

Fig. 39

(9)~(12) *Vedavrata Catuṣṭaya*

The HBKSam describes briefly the four Vedavratas which are considered to be four among sixteen Saṃskāras. They consist in following the observances while studying the four Kāṇḍas (i.e. chapters) of the Black Yajurveda. They are Prājāpatya, Saumya, Āgneya and Vaiśvadeva respectively.

According to the HBKSam, the agent of these performances is the teacher. The performance of the student is only on the instructions of the teacher. The beginning of the performance of each Vedavrata is fixed on an auspicious day after the Upanayana. Both the teacher and the student, after taking bath and performing their obligatory daily rites, sit facing the east and the teacher declares the purpose of the ritual. He performs the four preliminary rites. All the ceremonies from shaving the head up to the wearing of new gridle, holding a stuff etc., which are performed at the time of the Upanayana, are repeated once again and all the things which the Baṭu or student was wearing previously are thrown into the water. Then the teacher establishes the *laukika-agni* 'usual fire' and makes the student sit to his right. Then he offers six oblations of ghee to each of the seers of the Kāṇḍas, viz. to Prajāpati, Soma, Agni and Viśvadevas and also to the four deities (of the

Kāṇḍas). Then he gives oblations to Varuṇa, Agni and Prajāpati also. The student worships four deities, viz. Agni, Vāyu, Āditya and the Lord of the vows, making the promise of maintaining the performance of the vows.

On the completion of the study of each Kāṇḍa, i.e. of a Vedavrata, the teacher and the student again follow the same procedure which they have observed at the beginning of the first Vedavrata. At the end, the student worships four deities, viz. Agni etc., after he has fulfilled his promise successfully.

(13) Godāna

The Godāna Saṃskāra is performed in the 16th year, prior to the Samāvartana. The HBKSam says that Godāna is regarded as very much essential, like the Upanayana. Also HBKSam gives the etymology of the word Godāna in the following words:

> *gavi pṛthivyāṃ dīyante svāpārthaṃ yāni mastakasya catvāry aṅgāni teṣāṃ vapanādirūpaṃ karma godānakarmety ucyate* [HBKSam: 182B, 9]

The procedure and also the Mantras of this Saṃskāra are exactly the same as prescribed in the Caula. The only difference between the two rites lies in that in the Godāna, all the hair on the head, including the *śikhā* 'the top lock', are shaved (though the HirGS gives the option of retaining the top lock) while, in the Caula, the locks are arranged according to the tradition of the family.

Some other Gṛhyasūtras use the word *keśānta* for this rite and they mean to shave the beard and also the hair on the other parts of the body, viz. arm-pits. But neither HirGS nor the HBKSam, following the HirGS, mentions the shaving of the hair on the other parts of the body, but refers only to that on the head, and hence they have not made any distinction between the Caula and the Godāna rites.

(14) *Samāvartana*

The Samāvartana Saṃskāra, which literally means one's return to one's owning house from the teacher's house, signifies the termination point of the studentship. A student, having completed his course of study and having been permitted by his teacher, is required to perform this rite. The HirGS and the HBKSam supply astrological details for determining the proper time for the rite. They state that, during the northern course of the sun, in the bright half of a month and when the moon is in conjunction with a particular constellation, such as Rohiṇī etc., a student should take the ceremonial bath which is the prominent feature of this rite.

Fig. 40

The HirGS and also the HBKSam have stated an elaborate procedure of this rite. The student goes to a place which has water nearby and, performing *homa,* he offers oblations. He takes off his two garments, his stuff, the gridle, the black antelope-skin which he was wearing during his studentship and throws them into water. Then he shaves his beard, the hair under his arm-pits, the hair on his head and the body. Then he cuts off his nails and cleans his teeth with a stick of an Udumbara tree. He takes a bath with lukewarm water and anoints himself with sandal-wood paste. He wears a pair of new garments, puts on two ear-rings, ties the pellet around the neck and puts on a wreath. He looks in the mirror and takes up a stuff of reed. He rides on a chariot, or a horse, or an elephant and enters into a town. He goes to a place where he should get a hearty welcome and great honour. The host offers him the *madhuparka* 'mixture consisting of curds, honey and ghee.'

In modern times, this rite is quite simplified and a new feature is added to it. The student changes his clothes and leaves all the things which he was wearing from the time of the Upanayana. Perhaps the significance of the Marathi name of this rite *soḍamuñja* lies in giving up the gridle of Muñja grass which was tied around his waist on the day of the Upanayana. The boy pretends to go to Kāśī/Vārāṇasī on his proposed educational mission. He is persuaded by his maternal uncle for not going away, by promising to give him his daughter as a bride (see Fig. 40). The trend behind this promise can be traced to the regional social custom that a boy gets married with the daughter of his maternal uncle.

Also, the time of the Samāvartana rite is not observed according to the prescriptions of the Gṛhyasūtras. The Samāvartana which was to be performed at the completion of the study, is performed, nowadays, even on the same day of the Upanayana or on any day according to the convenience, even though the boy has not completed his studies. The implication behind this rite is almost lost today. As the marriage cannot take place before the Samāvartana, the latter is performed at a convenient time, but essentially before the marriage.

(15) *Vivāha*

Titles		*Fig Nos.*	*Divisions*
i.	*Ghāṇā*	—	xxxx
ii.	Four Preliminary Rites	—	xxx
iii.	*Maṇḍapadevatāpratiṣṭhā*	—	xxx
iv.	*Grahayajña*	41/42/43	xxx
v.	*Sīmāntapūjana*	44	xxx
vi.	*Vastradāna*	45	xxx
vii.	*Vāṅniścaya*	46	xx
viii.	*Telaphaḷa*	47	xxxx
ix.	*Gaurī-hara-pūjana*	48	xxx
x.	*Rukhavata*	49	xxxx
xi.	Welcoming the Bridegroom	50	xxxx
xii.	*Madhuparka*	51	xx
xiii.	Exchange of Garlands	52/53	xxxx
xiv.	*Kanyāpratipādana*	54/55	xx
xv.	*Kaṅkaṇa-bandhana*	56/57/58	xxx
xvi.	*Akṣatāropaṇa*	59/60	xxx
xvii.	*Maṅgalasūtra-bandhana*	61	xxx
xviii.	*Vivāhahoma*	62	xx
xix.	*Aśmārohaṇa*	63	xx
xx.	*Pāṇigrahaṇa*	64	xx
xxi.	*Lājāhoma*	65/66	xx
xxii.	*Agnipariṇayana*	67	xx

xxiii.	*Kānapilā*	68	xxxx
xiv.	*Saptapadī*	69	xx
xxv.	*Hṛdayasparśa*	70	xx
xxvi.	*Abhiṣeka*	71	xx
xxvii.	*Akṣatāropaṇa*	72	xxx
xxviii.	*Nakṣatradarśana*	73	xxx
xxix.	*Airaṇīpūjana*	74/75/76	xxx
xxx.	*Gṛhapraveśa*	77	xx
xxxi.	Welcoming the Couple	78	xxxx
xxxii.	*Lakṣmīpūjana*	79/80	xxx
xxxiii.	*Maṇḍapadevatotthāpana*	—	xxx
xxxiv.	*Satyanārāyaṇa Pūjā*	—	xxxx

[For divisions xx, xxx, xxxx, cf. under Upanayana.]

(i) *Ghāṇā*, see Upanayana (p.113) above.

(ii) Four Preliminary Rites, see Introduction (pp.94-99) above.

(iii) *Maṇḍapadevatāpratiṣṭhā*, see Upanayana (p.114) above.

(iv) *Grahayajña*

This ritual is an invocation to all the deities and invitation to them for their smoothly leading the Vivāha ceremony, dispelling away all the evils and calamities. This rite is performed on the occasion of the Upanayana ceremony also.

The Yajamāna appoints one priest in charge of the entire ritual. He scatters mustard seeds in all directions with a view to dispelling (or, warding away) the calamities and consecrates the material for the ritual by sprinkling water over the same. He prepares a special seat for the planets in the middle of which he draws the sun. Then, facing the east, he draws with the red flowers and in the south-east direction he draws the moon, facing the west with white flowers. He places the planet Mars in the south direction, Mercury in the north-east direction, Jupiter in the north, Venus in the east, Saturn in the west, Rāhu in the south-west and Ketu in the north-west. He invokes and invites the respective deities and worships them with *ṣoḍaśopacāras*. He kindles the fire called *varada* and establishes it in the south-west direction. He puts into the fire eight offerings for each of the deities. Then he offers a *bali* 'oblation' to all the deities and invites the Kṣetrapālas and worships them with the offering of oblations. He pleases all the deities and divine beings by this ritual. At the end, the priest consecrates the Yajamāna and his family by sprinkling water.

Fig. 41b

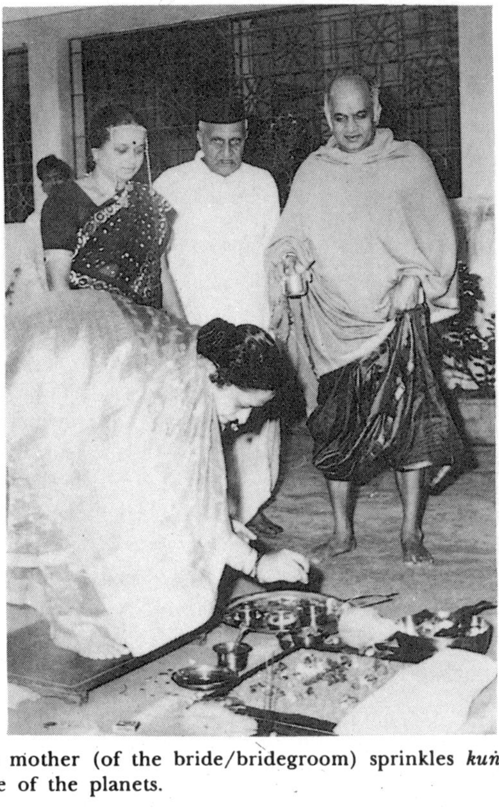

Fig. 42 The mother (of the bride/bridegroom) sprinkles *kuṅkuma* on the figure of the planets.

Fig. 43 She offers a coconut to the planets.

(v) *Sīmāntapūjana*

Sīmāntapūjana literally means welcoming and honouring the bridegroom and his relatives on their arrival at the entrance or gate of the city (*sīmānta*) of the bride. In modern times, it is the first ceremony performed in the Vivāha. It takes place in the evening or night before the day of the Vivāha. It is traditional that the groom comes to the house/town of the bride for the Vivāha and the father of the bride receives him at the gate.

> *caraṇaṃ pavitraṃ vitataṃ purāṇam/ yena pūtas tarati duṣkṛtāni/ tena pavitreṇa śuddhena pūtāḥ/ ati pāpmānam arātiṃ tarema/*
> [HBKSam:191A, 5(brief), completed by Apteji]
> "May we overcome the sin(s) and the enemy (enemies), being purified by (the touch of) that pure and holy foot—thereby, i.e. by that holy foot, extending (over the sky), the ancient one, one is able to overcome (all) evils, being purified (oneself)." [Cf. Vāmana's foot which occupies the whole of the Universe.]

Fig. 44 The father of the bride, having welcomed the bridegroom, offers him a seat and washes his feet, while the mother (standing on the left of her husband) pours water on the feet.

(vi) *Vastradāna*

Fig. 45 The father of the bride presents new clothes to the groom. Then he garlands the groom. [= See Fig. 4 above]

(vii) *Vāṅniścaya*

The HBKSam records this ceremony as *Vāgdāna.* This ceremony, as the name literally signifies, is the confirmation of the wedding as agreed by the fathers of both, the bride and the bridegroom. It is performed after the *Sīmāntapūjana* on the same night (i.e. one day before the wedding). But the HBKSam describes this ceremony after *Kanyāvaraṇa,* before *Sīmāntapūjana* etc., which means that the settlement of wedding should be before the bridegroom's coming to the house of the bride.

Fig. 46 The father of the bride, with the bride sitting to his left, sits facing the father of the groom. He worships Gaṇapati and Varuṇa. Then he honours the father of the groom by applying *gandha* 'sandal-wood paste' on his forehead and gives betel-nut leaves and a betel-nut to him.

phalena phalitaṃ sarvaṃ trailokyaṃ sacarācaram/ tasmāt phalapradānena saphalāś ca manorathāḥ [narrated by Aptеji] "The three-worlds, together with the sentient (beings) and the insentient (things) in them, are said to have borne fruit when there appears the fruit (of each one of them). Therefore, by giving this fruit to you our wishes (in performing this wedding) are fulfilled."

Then the father of the bride, putting a piece of turmeric and five betel-nuts, ties a knot at the end of the upper garment of the father of the groom and pronounces these words: 'I give this girl, born in such and such family and of such and such persons, named so and so, to the boy who is born in such and such family, great grandson, grandson and son of such and such persons!' The father of the groom confirms that he has accepted that offer in the same manner.

(viii) *Telaphaḷa*

Telaphaḷa is a Marathi word and it signifies a rite, peculiar to some families only. The bride and her mother sit in front of the goddess *Gaurī* (who is worshipped by the bride before wedding, i.e. before the recitation of *maṅgalāṣṭakas* and exchanging of garlands). The mother of the groom washes the feet of the bride and of her mother with warm water. Then she gives a green saree to the bride and a saree or a piece of cloth to her mother. At the same time, she gives the bride silver rings which are worn on the second and the fourth fingers of the feet. Five ladies of the house offer rice-grains along with a variety of fruits to the bride.

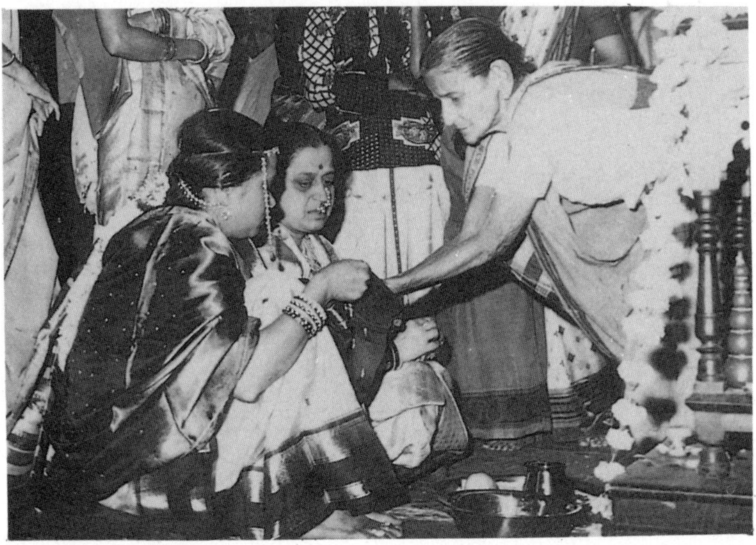

Fig. 47 A lady offers rice-grains along with fruits.

(ix) *Gaurī-Hara-Pūjana*

This custom is mentioned in the medieval texts; it is prevalent in the modern times also. It is a worship of *gaurīhara*, viz. Gaurī (Śiva's consort) and Śiva, it also is the worship of Śacī, the consort of Indra. The bride worships an image of Gaurī with a desire of good fortune, prosperity and happiness before proceeding to the place of the wedding, (i.e. to the place where there will be the recitation of Maṅgalāṣṭakas and exchange of garlands).

Fig. 48

devendrāṇi namas tubhyaṃ devendrapriyabhāmini/ vivāhaṃ bhāgyam ārogyam putralābhaṃ ca dehi me// [HBKSam:191B, 5] "Salutation to you, O wife of Indra, O beloved of Indra; (please) bless me with (lit. grant unto) me (a happy) wedding, fortune, health and the boon of a son."

(x) *Rukhavata*

The mother of the bride goes to invite the groom and, at that time, makes an offering of eatables to the groom, his friends and others. Before going to the bride's house for the wedding, the groom, together with his relatives and friends, takes meals. This is, of course, a social custom. Then the bridegroom goes to the bride's house.

Fig. 49 The mother of the bride pours ghee on the palm of the groom after he has finished his meals.

(xi) Welcoming the Bridegroom

When the groom arrives at the house of the bride for the wedding,

Fig. 50

the mother of the bride welcomes him at the door by washing his feet. Also she waves a lamp around his face.

(xii) *Madhuparka*

When the groom arrives at the house of the bride, the parents of the bride welcome him and offer him *Madhuparka*, an honour, reserved for the distinguished persons in the society. They offer him a seat and then a mixture of honey, curds and ghee. The groom eats this mixture. This is performed for three times. In the Ṛgvedic tradition, the three offerings to the groom are accompanied by three different Mantras, while in the Hiraṇyakeśī tradition, the same Mantra is repeated.

Fig. 51

tejase tvā śriyai yaśase balāyānnādyāya prāśnāmi [HBKSam: 187B, 10]

"I drink you for lustre, wealth, fame, strength and food."

After the rite of *Madhuparka* is over, the Brāhmaṇas place two wooden planks, with small heaps of rice-grains on them, side by side. The groom stands on the wooden plank facing the east whereas the bride stands on the other which is facing the west. A piece of cloth is held between them. The eight auspicious verses called *maṅgalāṣṭakas* are recited by the Brāhmaṇas. The relatives who have gathered around the couple sprinkle rice grains on their head for blessing after the completion. (See Fig. 25 above) At the auspicious moment, which is fixed according to the astrology, the cloth held between the bridegroom and the bride is removed. Then they exchange garlands.

(xiii) Exchange of Garlands

Fig. 52 The bride garlands the groom.

Fig. 53 The groom garlands the bride.

(xiv) *Kanyāpratipādana*

All other Gṛhyasūtras and other texts on the Saṃskāras as well refer to this rite as *Kanyādāna*, i.e. the gift of the bride. But, in the *saṃkalpa* of this rite, the HBKSam mentions it as *Kanyāpratipādana*. The father expresses his wish to give his daughter to the groom who is (taken by him as) none else than god Viṣṇu. Then, together with his wife, he stands facing the eastern direction and, touching the right shoulder of the bride recites this Mantra:

kanyāṃ kanakasaṃpannāṃ kanakābharaṇair yutām/
dāsyāmi viṣṇave tubhyaṃ brahmalokajigīṣayā//
viśvambhara sarvabhūtāḥ sākṣiṇyaḥ sarvadevatāḥ/
imāṃ kanyām pradāsyāmi pitṝṇāṃ tāraṇāya ca//
[HBKSam:193B, 1-2]

"With a wish to secure the world of Brahmadeva, I offer you, O Viṣṇu, my daughter decked in gold and golden ornaments, O you god, who nourish this Universe, who have been all (this world) and who witness (all that happens here), I shall offer (my daughter to this bridegroom) for gratifying the Pitṛs."

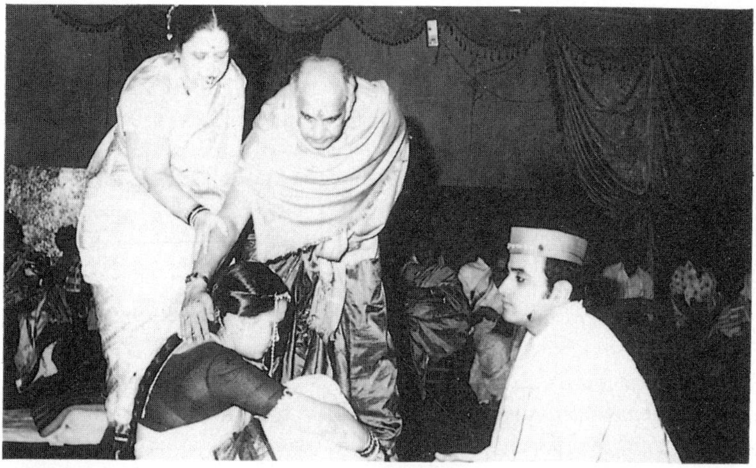

Fig. 54

Fig. 55

The newly-wed couple and the parents of the bride stand face to face with each other. The bridegroom and the bride hold both their palms, placed one upon the other above a slightly hollowed copper plate. The mother of the bride continuously pours water on the right palm of the father. It flows down into the palms of the groom which are placed just above the palms of the bride. Then, the water which comes down from the palms of the groom and of the bride, is gathered in the copper plate.

> *amukapravaropetāmamukagotrotpannāyāmukaprapautrāya amukapautrāyāmukaputrāyāmukaśarmaṇe kanyārthine śrīdhara-rūpiṇe varāya/ amukapravaropetāmamukagotrotpannāmamuka-prapautrīm amukapautrīm amukaputrīm amukanāmnīṃ kanyāṃ varārthinīṃ śrīrūpiṇīṃ prajāpatidaivatyāṃ prajāsahatvakarmabhyas tubhyam ahaṃ pratipādaye/*
> "I give unto you, the bridegroom of such and such *pravara*, of such and such *gotra*, great grandson of such and such person, grandson of such and such person, son of such and such person, of such and such name, wishing for my daughter (as your bride), O Lord Śrīdhara incarnate, my daughter, born in such and such *pravara* and *gotra*, great granddaughter of such and such person, granddaughter of such and such person, daughter of such and such person, of such and such name, this young girl, wishing for a husband, the goddess Śrī incarnate, having Prajāpati as her deity, so that she cooperates in your religious duty of procreation."

The groom accepts her formally with the words *tathā* 'be it so'. This is said (and done) thrice. Before concluding, the father puts forward the following condition to the groom: 'In respect of Dharma, wealth and desire, she is not to be transgressed (by you).' On this, the groom promises, 'I shall not transgress her.' For the fulfilment of this rite, the father gives the *dakṣiṇā* in the form of gold, money and other presents. [HBKSam:193B,6-194A,2]

(xv) *Kaṅkaṇa-bandhana*

The groom and the bride sit, facing each other. The Brāhmaṇas encircle a white thread dipped in the milk around their necks and also around their waists for four or five times with the recitation of the Mantras.

Fig. 56

The thread which was encircled around the necks is removed from the legs in the downward direction. A piece of turmeric is tied in it and the groom ties the same on the left wrist of the bride A Mantra is recited at that time. [HBKSam:194B, 10-11]

Fig. 57

Fig. 58

The thread encircled around the waists is removed from the upper direction (i.e. from the upper part of the body) and a piece of turmeric is tied in it, as stated above. It is tied on the right fore-arm (i.e. wrist) of the groom by the bride with a Mantra. [HBKSam: 194B, 12-13]

(xvi) *Akṣatāropaṇa* 'mutual showering of rice-grains by turns'

Fig. 59 The bride pours rice-grains on the head of the groom.

Fig. 60 The groom also pours the rice-grains on the head of the bride.

The Mantras are:

(1) bride: *bhago me kāmaḥ samṛddhyatām/*
"Fortune is my desire. May it flourish (i.e. be fulfilled)."
groom: *yajño me kāmaḥ samṛddhyatām/*
"Sacrifice ...."

(2) bride: *śriyo me kāmaḥ samṛddhyatām/*
"Wealth...."
groom: *dharmo me kāmaḥ samṛddhyatām/*
"Merit...."

(3) bride: *prajā me kāmaḥ samṛddhyatām/*
"Offspring...."
groom: *yaśo me kāmaḥ samṛddhyatām/*
"Fame...."

These three showerings are repeated again. [HBKSam:195A, 4-9]

This rite is performed with a desire for a long and prosperous life. Milk of a cow is poured in a silver vessel and clarified butter is sprinkled over it. The groom applies the milk and ghee to the joined palms of the bride twice. Then he puts on it rice-grains, thrice and sprinkles them with the milk mixed with the ghee. Someone else does the same procedure for the groom. The bride pours the rice-grains on the head of the bridegroom and *vice-versa.*

During this pouring, they express their wish in the same way *bhago me ...* For the seventh time, the bride pours the rice-grains silently (*tuṣṇīṃ kāryam*). [HBKSam: 195, 9-10]

(xvii) *Maṅgalasūtra-bandhana*

There is a custom, for a wife, to wear a *maṅgalasūtra* in the middle and the southern parts of India. So long as her husband is alive, she wears it and, at his demise, she has to remove it off and the *vaṭī* 'the central hollow half-bead (of gold)' and the golden beads are to be burnt with the dead body of the husband. The Sūtras are, however, silent about this tradition. After tying up the *maṅgalasūtra* (before the *Vivāhahoma*) the newly-weds perform *Gaṇapatipūjana, Lakṣmī-pārvatī* and *śacīpūjana*. This is done with a view to keeping up and strengthening the vows of Vivāha. [cf. HBKSam:195B, 1-5] The *Gaṇapatipūjana*, at the beginning (in *Devadevaka*) up to *Kanyāpratipādana*, forms one unit, the rites are performed by the parents. Afterwards, the couple performs their rites independently, i.e. by themselves.

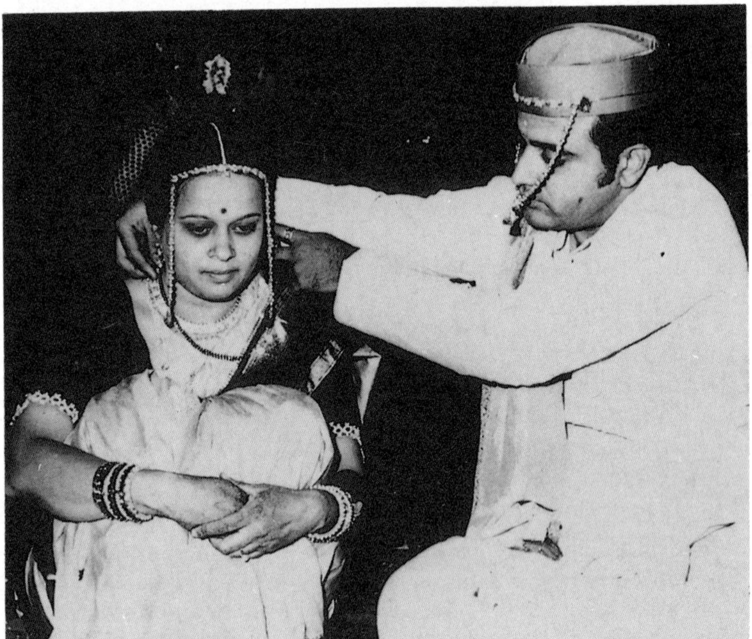

Fig. 61 The couple sits facing the east. The mother-in-law gives a saree to the bride and the groom ties the string, in which black beads are inserted, around her neck.

māṅgalyatantunānena bhartṛjīvanahetunā/ kaṇṭhe badhnāmi subhage sā jīva śaradāṃ śatam// [HBKSam:195A, 13]

"I bind around your neck this auspicious thread, the source of (your) husband's life, O charming one; thus may you live for a hundred autumns."

(xviii) *Vivāhahoma*

The couple then performs the *Vivāhahoma.* Following the Mantras, the husband offers six oblations (*ṣaḍ-āhutis*) of ghee in correspondence with the recitaion of six Mantras. [HBKSam:196B, 5-6(brief)] The bride touches his right hand with her right hand which means that she is also participating in the rite.

The text of the HirGS mentions this sacrifice as the first rite of the Vivāha Saṃskāra. All the preceding rites are either customary or added by the Prayoga-texts, trying to incorporate the local tradition(s).

Fig. 62

(xix) *Aśmārohaṇa*

After the six oblations are offered into the fire, the bride goes to the north-west direction of the fire and treads on a stone. This action is symbolic. It signifies the firm devotion and the steadfast position of the wife in the family (which resembles the firmness of a stone) in the future life. As the bride mounts on the stone, the following Mantra is recited:

> *ā tiṣṭhemam aśmānam aśmeva tvaṃ sthirā bhava/ pra mṛṇīhi durasyūnt sahasva pṛtanāyate//* [HBKSam:196B, 7-8]
>
> "Step on this stone; be steady like (this) stone. Strike down those who unite with evils (and) overcome those who bear enmity."

Fig. 63

(xx) *Pāṇigrahaṇa*

The groom stands, facing the west, in front of the bride and holds her right hand together with the thumb in the upward position. The Gṛhyasūtra adds, if the husband desires to generate a male child, he is supposed to seize her thumb, and if a female child, her other fingers. If he desires both male and female progany, he seizes the thumb together with other fingers. Then he makes her move and asks her to stand on his left side. Holding her right shoulder, he recites the Mantras:

> *sarasvati predam iva subhage vājinīvati/ tāṃ tvā viśvasya bhūtasya prajāyām asy agrataḥ/ gṛhṇāmi te suprajāstvāya hastaṃ mayā patyā jaradaṣṭir yathāsat/ bhago aryamā savitā puraṃdhir mahyaṃ tvādur gārhapatyāya devāḥ//* [HBKSam:196B, 11-12]

"Sarasvatī! Promote this (our understanding), O gracious one, rich in studs,* you, whom we sing first of all that is.
I seize your hand that we may be blessed with offspring, that you may live to old age with me, your husband. Bhaga, Aryaman, Savitṛ, Purandhi, the gods have given you to me that we may rule our house." [SBE:189]

* Yet, the modern translation could be, 'possessing rich (or strength-giving) foods'

He makes her turn round, from left to right, so that she faces the west, and recites the Mantra.

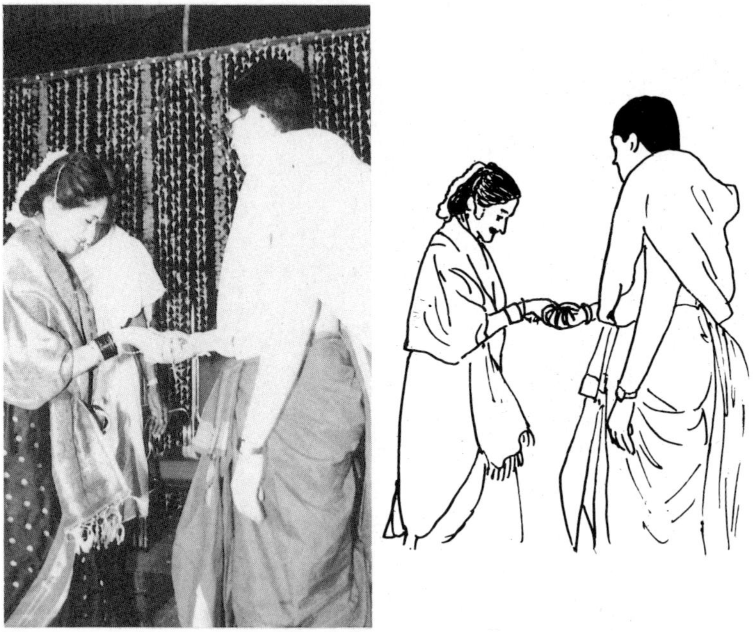

Fig. 64a~64b Seizing of the bride's hand

(xxi) *Lājāhoma*

This *homa* is called *Lājāhoma*, for they use *lājas* 'fried rice-grains' as an offering.

Fig. 65 The couple sits in front of the fire. The groom sprinkles ghee into the bride's joined palms with the Mantra stated below and her brother puts fried rice-grains into her palms twice, thrice or five times.

imān lājān ā vapāmi samṛddhikaraṇān mama tubhyaṃ ca saṃvananaṃ tad agnir anumanyatām ayam//
[HBKSam:197A, 5-6]
"This grain I pour (into thy hands): may it bring prosperity to me, and may it unite you with me. May this Agni grant us that."[SBE:190]

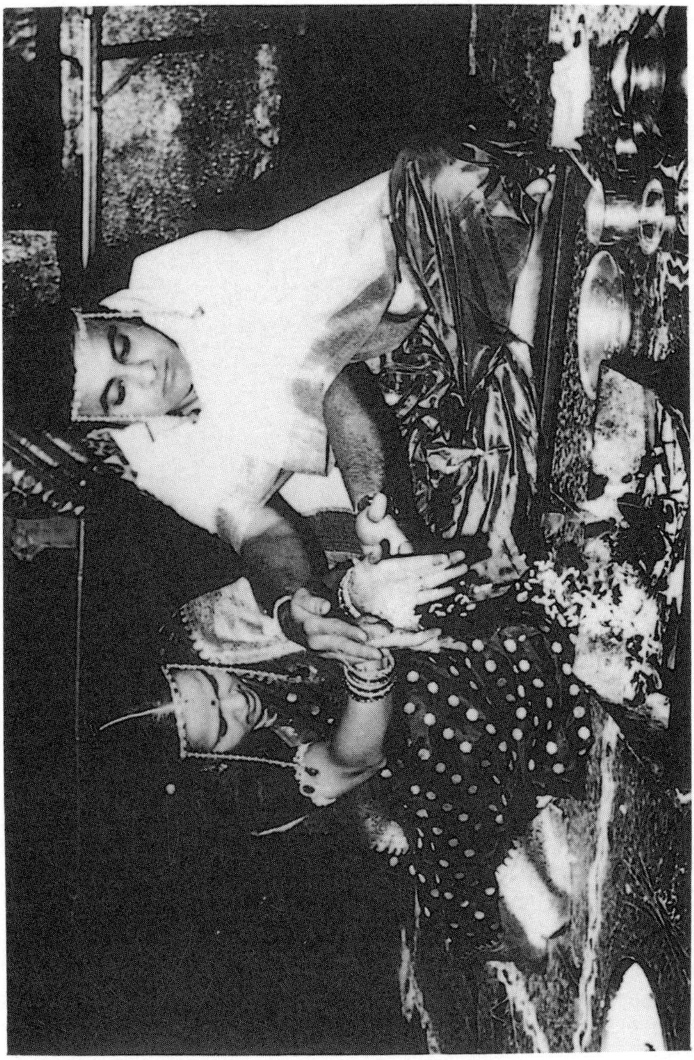

Fig. 66 The groom again sprinkles ghee on the fried rice-grains in the palms of the bride, and, holding her palms, he pours them into the fire.

(xxii) *Agnipariṇayana*

After making these oblations, both of them stand up. While the recitation of Mantras is going on, the groom holds the right hand of the bride and both of them circumambulate the fire (*pradakṣiṇā*)—[HBKSam:197A, 7-9]

The procedure performed in Figs. 65-66-67 is adopted thrice.

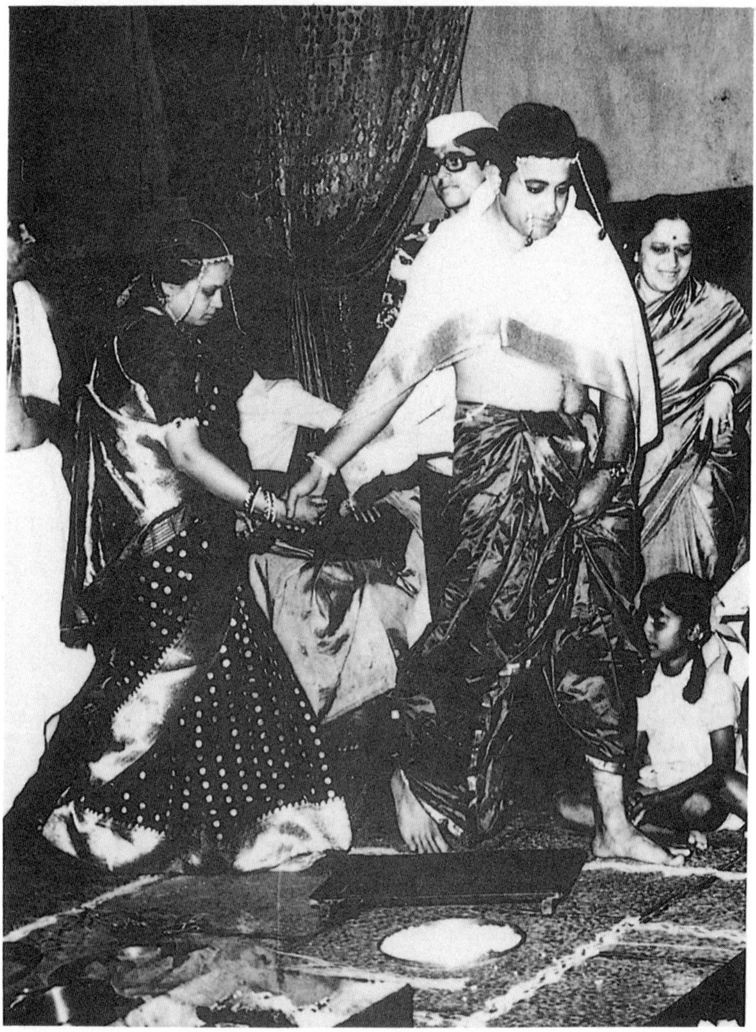

Fig. 67

(xxiii) *Kānapiḷā*

This is purely a social custom (i.e. not accompanied by any Mantra). The brother of the bride holds the right ear of the groom with a view to warning him to take good care of his sister. And, on this, the groom gives a gift to the brother-in-law.

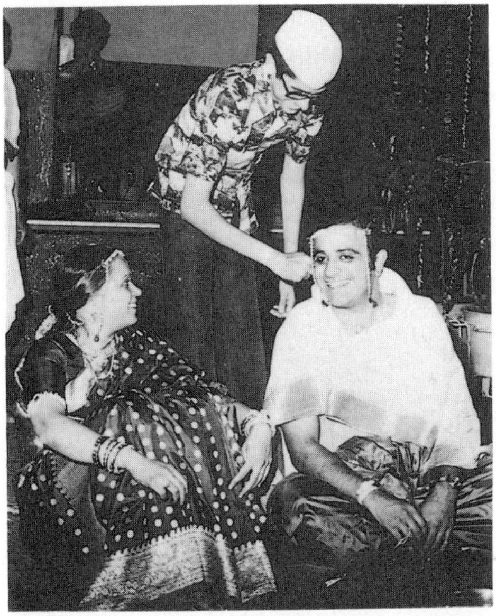

Fig. 68 A brother of the bride holds the right ear of the groom.

(xxiv) *Saptapadī*

The bride steps her right foot on each of the seven heaps of rice-grains in the northern direction and her action is accompanied by Mantras. The groom walks along with her, keeping his right hand on her right shoulder.

ekam iṣe viṣṇus tvānvetu/
dve urje viṣṇus tvānvetu/
trīṇi vratāya viṣṇus tvānvetu/
catvāri māyobhavāya viṣṇus tvānvetu/
pañca paśubhyo viṣṇus tvānvetu/
saḍ rāyaspoṣāya viṣṇus tvānvetu/
sapta saptabhyo hotrābhyo viṣṇus tvānvetu/ sakhāyau saptapadāvabhūva sakhyaṃ te gameyaṃ sakhyāt te mā yoṣaṃ sakhyān me mā yoṣṭhāḥ/ [HBKSam:197B, 2-5]

"One (step) for sap, may Viṣṇu go after thee; two (steps) for juice, may Viṣṇu go after thee; three (steps) for vows, may Viṣṇu go after thee; four (steps) for comfort, may Viṣṇu go after thee; five (steps) for cattles may Viṣṇu go after thee; six (steps) for prospering, may Viṣṇu go after thee; seven (steps) for sevenfold Hotṛship, may Viṣṇu go after thee. With seven steps we have become friends. May I attain to friendship with thee. May I not be separated from thy friendship. Mayst thou not be separated from my friendship." [SBE:192]

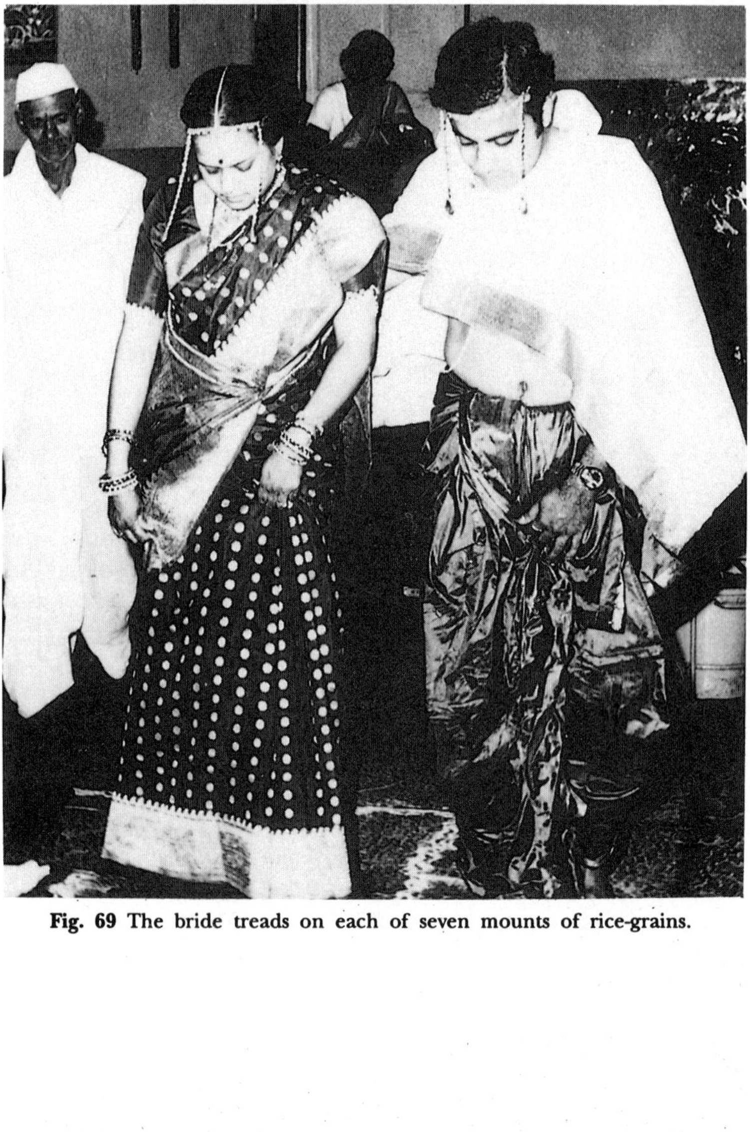

Fig. 69 The bride treads on each of seven mounts of rice-grains.

(xxv) *Hṛdayasparśa*

After *Saptapadī* 'walking seven steps together', the groom first touches her heart and then her navel, reciting the following Mantra:

mama hṛdaye hṛdayaṃ te astu mama cittaṃ cittenānvehi mama vācam ekamanā juṣasva bṛhaspatis tvā niyunaktu mahyaṃ mām evānusaṃrabhasva mayi cittāni santu te mayi sāmīcyam astu te mahyaṃ vācaṃ niyacchatāt/ [HBKSam:197B, 6-7]

"May your heart be fixed in my heart; follow my mind with your mind; enjoy my speech with the whole of your mind. May Bṛhaspati govern (lit. employ) you for me (i.e. to render service/help to me); follow my act in your act; may your thought be fixed on me; may you be wholly attached to me. May you govern your speech for me."

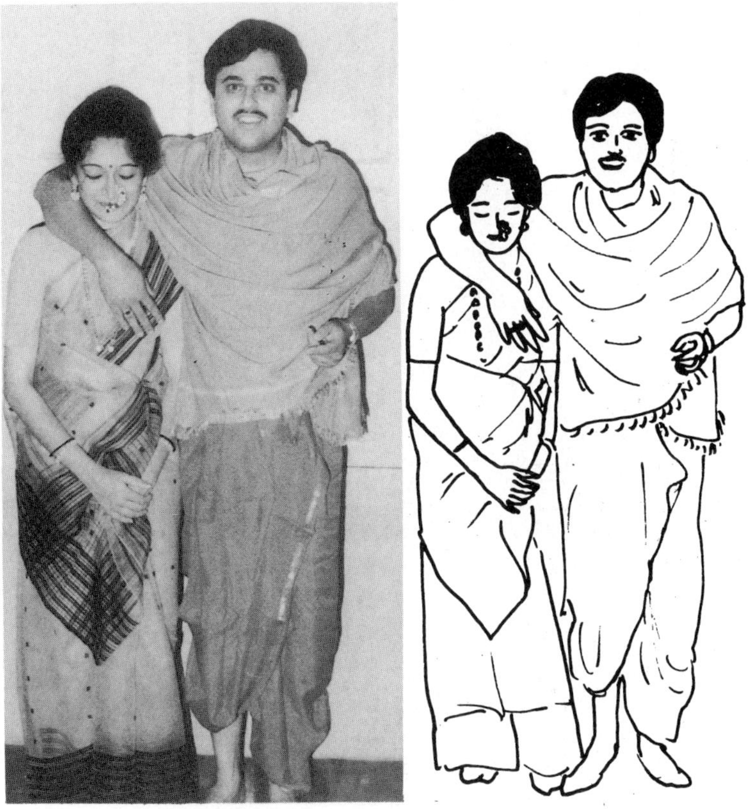

Fig. 70a~70b Touching the heart of the bride.

(xxvi) *Abhiṣeka*

The bride sits facing the east and the groom stands in front of her, facing the west. He sprinkles the water from the pot with the Kuśa grass, recites the seven Mantras and an *anuvāka*. [HBKSam:197B, 8-9 (brief)]

Fig. 71 The groom sprinkles water on her.

(xxvii) *Akṣatāropaṇa*

While the Mantras (for the preceding) are recited, the Brāhmaṇas and the elderly persons scatter rice-grains on the head of bride, for blessing. [HBKSam:197B, 9-10]

Hereafter, there is no description of rites in the HBKSam. But it is stated that whatever is traditionally accepted is to be performed. [HBKSam:197B, 10-11]

After coming to their home (i.e. house of the groom), the newly-wed couple brings the *Vivāhāgni* 'the fire which was kindled at the time of *Vivāhahoma*' and establishes it as the *gṛhyāgni*. It was so prescribed in older times (in Gṛhya texts), but nowadays this rite is not performed, for none carries the *Vivāhāgni* to the house.

Fig. 72

(xxviii) *Nakṣatradarśana*

When the stars appear in the sky, the groom takes the bride outside the house and, facing to the northern direction, he shows her the polar star. As the polar star is steady in the northern direction, so should the couple also be firm/steady in their future life—such is the wish implied.

In modern times, this customary rite is performed immediately after the *Vivāhahoma* is completed. Obviously, it is performed before the bride enters the house of the groom, i.e. at the household of her father.

Fig. 73a~73b Watching the constellation called the seven ṛṣis and the polar star.

(xxix) *Airiṇīpūjana*

This rite means the worship of the groom and his mother. The parents of the bride honour the bridegroom's mother and other relatives of the groom by presenting them gifts in accordance with their statuses.

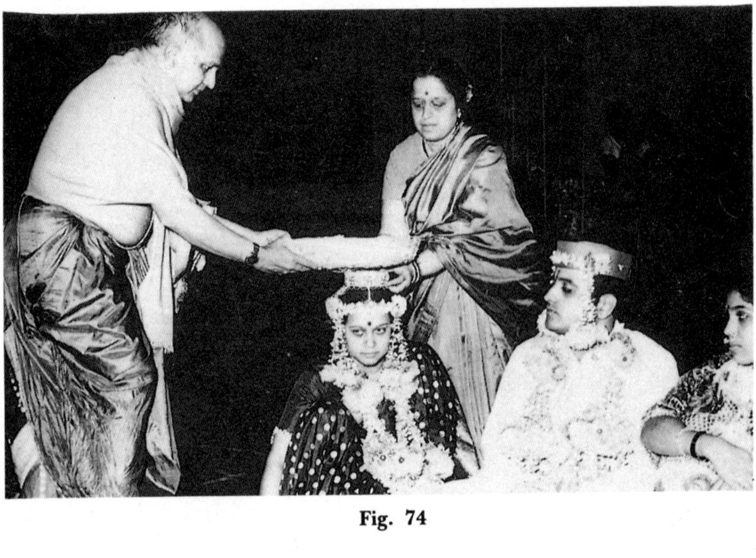

Fig. 74

The parents of the bride put a round basket of bamboo, in which small lamps are lighted, first on the head of the bride—indicating the responsibility on her in her future life. The basket of bamboo is significant, as it is held to symbolize the continuation of the family of the bridegroom.

Fig. 75

They put the same basket on the heads of the elderly persons from the groom's household. This signifies that the responsibility of their daughter, henceforth, lies on them.

Fig. 76a

Fig. 76b

The father of the bride requests that the full responsibility of their daughter is shifted to the parents of the groom and that they should take care of her.

saptavarṣā tv iyaṃ kanyā putravat pālitā mayā/ idānīṃ tava putrāya dattā snehena pālyatām// [HBKSam:200B, 13]
"This girl of seven years, is brought up by me, like a son—she is now given to your son; take care of her, with affection."

After the ceremony in the morning and before the *Lakṣmīpūjana* at night, there are, only social customs, both the reception and *devadarśana.* After the wedding ceremony is over, the custom in Pune is that the couple visits the temples of Kasabā Gaṇapati and Jogeśvarī, which are regarded as the *grāmadevatās.* The parents of the groom and also of the bride had offered the invitation to Kasabā Gaṇapati before delivering the invitation cards to relatives and friends. We can thus notice the role of the *grāmadevatā* on the occasion of Vivāha.

(xxx) *Gṛhapraveśa*

The couple then enters the house of the groom. The bride puts off the vessel full of rice-grains with her right foot, while she steps across the threshhold of the house.

Fig. 77

(xxxi) Welcoming the Couple

The mother of the groom welcomes the couple by waving a lamp around their heads.

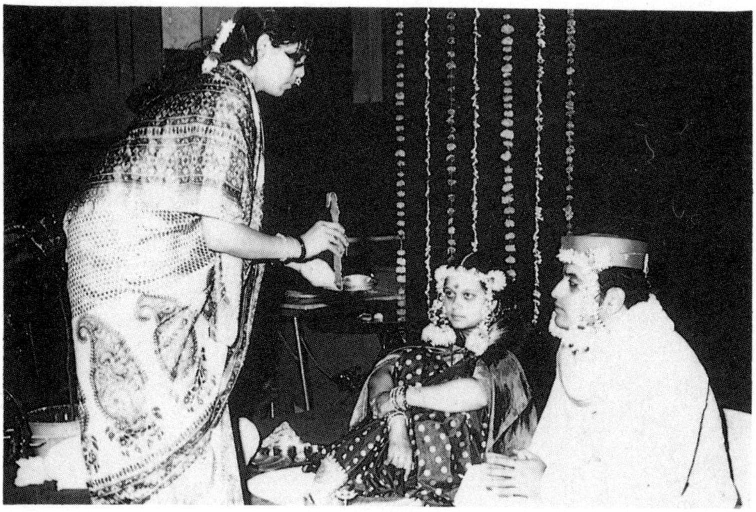

Fig. 78

(xxxii) *Lakṣmīpūjana*

The model of this rite is taken from the *Nāmakaraṇavidhi.*

Fig. 79

Before naming the bride in the new household, worship is offered to Gaṇapati (as in the Nāmakaraṇavidhi) and to goddess Lakṣmī. The bride is, at this moment, being honoured as Lakṣmī of the household.

Fig. 80

The groom writes the name of the bride (in the new household) on rice-grains in a plate.

Before announcing the name of the newly-wed bride to the public, the groom tells it into the right ear of the bride.

(xxxiii) *Maṇḍapadevatotthāpana,* see Upanayana (p. 130) above

(xxxiv) *Satyanārāyaṇa Pūjā,* see Upanayana (p.131) above.

(16) *Antyeṣṭi*

Antyeṣṭi 'funeral rite' is the last Saṃskāra, performed on the human body. The HBKSam [377B] describes, prior to the procedure funeral, a rite called *sarvaprāyaścitta* 'expiatory rite for destroying all types of sins or offences done by the dead person, either knowingly or unknowingly'. When a person feels that death is approaching him, he should perform this rite with a view to getting released from the bond of sin or guilt and to purifying his own self; in it he makes a gift of a cow to a Brāhmaṇa. If he is unable to give a cow, he gives money in lieu of it. Various types of gifts are prescribed for different types of sins.

As the description of the HBKSam reads, it can be noticed that funeral rites and the rites after death show variations in the cases of different persons, viz. in the case of an *āhitāgni*, one who has kindled a *smārta* fire only, of a person who had no fire of all, of an ascetic, of a woman etc.

In modern times, the funeral rite is performed according to the Paddhati texts following the *Pitṛmedhasūtras*. Of course, these later texts supply some details and introduce few changes in the original procedure. The relatives purify the body of the deceased with a bath at home and cover it with new garments. The son of the dead person performs a Śrāddha before taking the dead body to the cremation ground. He offers a *piṇḍa* to the dead and keeps it on his arm. Then the corpse is tied on the bier made of bamboo. The relatives, mostly the sons or the blood-relations, of that person carry the corpse to the cremation ground. The funeral procession is headed by the chief mourner, usually the eldest son of the dead, carrying the fire, which had been kindled as the domestic fire, in his hand to the cremation ground for performing the last rites. The funeral bier is followed by the relatives and the friends.

When a person dies, his son or, other relative, declares his resolve to perform the funeral rites of that person, born in such and such *gotra*, with a view to his getting released from the state of *pretatva* and to attain to the world of Pitṛs. He goes to the site in the cremation ground prepared as per the measurements laid down by the Gṛhyasūtras and the Pitṛmedhasūtras, and sprinkles water on the ground with either a *palāśa* branch or a *śamī* branch. He throws the branch of the tree to his right, touches the water and sprinkles it. Then he puts some gold on that ground and gets the funeral pile (of wood) prepared. Then he goes around the place, dug up for cremation, thrice, spreads Darbha and/or Kuśa grass. He fills the jar with water mixed with various herbs and cleanses the dead body. Then the relatives put the dead body on the funeral pile (placing the head to the south). The son puts gold, or drops of clarified butter substituting the gold, on various parts of the body of the dead, reciting various Mantras. He prepares the *piṇḍas* and places them on the five parts, viz. the forehead, eyes, two arms, the navel and legs. Or, alternatively, he prepares three *piṇḍas* and places them on the forehead, chest and navel. Then he sets to fire the pile, towards the head, if the deceased is male, and towards the feet, if it is a female. After the pile is set to burning, he takes a jar full of water on his left shoulder, makes a hole in it with a stone and, sprinkling water, goes around the burning body with his left towards the pile. He performs this action thrice. He breaks the jar completely near the head of the burning body. The relatives, headed by the younger members, come away from the cremation ground, without looking around. They go to a place near water, get their hair and beard shaved and take bath. They turn their faces towards the south and, calling the name of the dead person, offer a handful of water to him. When they arrive at their homes, at the door, they chew the leaves of a Neem tree and, headed by the younger ones, they enter the house.

In the house a lamp is kept burning, continously for ten days, on the ground where the death had occurred. From the first day up to the tenth day, water and milk or handful of rice in the separate bowls are kept in the open space of the house at the time of mid-day meals as food for the deceased. The implication of this offering is that it serves the *pātheya* 'food one the journey (to the land of the Pitṛs)' of the departed soul. He can take bath with the water and drink milk on his way to the Pitṛloka.

The rite that follows the cremation is *asthisaṃcayana* 'collection of bones'. It is performed on the next day of the cremation or on the third, or the fifth or the seventh day. The performer sprinkles, with an *udumbara* branch on the bones, milk mixed with water, and offers three oblations to Agni. Then he collects bones—the bones of the head being collected first and those of the feet last, puts them in an urn and offers Śrāddha to the departed one. In modern times, the bones are collected just after the cremation and, together with the ashes, they are cast in the water of a river nearby. Some people go either to some sacred place or (even) to the river Ganges for casting the ashes into them.

The Prayoga-texts prescribe various offerings to the dead during the Āśauca period. They contain the offerings from the first day after the death to the ninth day. The dead is regarded as a live. Therefore, these offerings are implied to provide him with food and to help him to be endowed with a new body, for going to the other world, as his old body was burnt in this world. Each oblation specifies a new limb in succession.

On the tenth day, all the blood-relations and other relatives gather on the banks of the river for offering the water to the deceased. They take a handful of water mixed with sesame and, allowing the water to flow downwards from their right thumb, pour it on the piece of the stone with which the water-jar was cracked at the time of cremation. (It is believed that the 'life' element of the departed has been lying in that stone.)

The performer places five small pots full of water and five rice-balls on them. They are meant for quenching the hunger and the thurst of the departed, his friends, Vaivasvata Yama, the crow and Rudra respectively. Traditionally, people wait till the crow eats (or at least touches) the rice-ball. (It is believed that, if the crow touches the rice-balls, all the desires of the departed are taken to have been fulfilled. But if a person is dead, with some unfulfilled desire in his mind, the crow would not turn up!) Then the performer casts the piece of stone into the water of the river and all of them return home.

Abbreviations

HBKSam	*Hiraṇyakeśibrahmakarmasamuccaya*
SBE	English translation of the *Hiraṇyakeśigṛhyasūtra*
Paddhati	*Saṃskārāpaddhati*
HirGS	*Hiraṇyakeśigṛhyasūtra*

[See the following pages for their bibliographical notes]

Bibliography

Abhyankar, Vasudeva Shastri (ed.) [abbr. Paddhati]

1924 *Saṃskārapaddhati*. Ānanda Āśrama Sanskrit Series 94. Poona: Ānanda Āśrama Mudrā Ālaya.

Aiyangar, S. Krishnasvami (ed.)

1940 *Paramasaṃhitā*. Gaekwad's Oriental Series 86. Baroda: Oriental Institute.

Apte, Mahadev Cimanaj (ed.)

1948 *Kṛṣṇayajurvedīyataittirīyasaṃhitā*, Part 6. Ānanda Āśrama Sanskrit Series 42. Poona: Ānanda Āśrama Mudrā Ālaya.

Apte, Vaman Shivaram

1978 *The Practical Sanskrit-English Dictionary* (reprt.). Kyoto: Rinsen Book Company.

Aufrecht, Theodor (ed.)

1968 *Die Hymnen des Ṛgveda*. Wiesbaden: Otto Harrassowitz. (vierter Auflage).

Charpentier, Jarl

1927 The Meaning and Etymology of Pūjā. *The Indian Antiquary* LVL, pp. 93–98, 130–135.

Citrav, S.

1977a *Samdhyā*. Poona: Bharatiya Caritrakoś Mandala.

1977b *Pūjā*. Poona: Bharatiya Caritrakoś Mandala.

Dandge, G. B.

1977 *Śrīgaṇapati Atharvaśīrṣa*. Kolhapur: Maharashtra Grantha Bhandara.

Dev, H. N.

1969 *Śrīdevī Upāsanā āṇi Gāyatrīmahātmya*. Poona: Kshīrasāgar Āṇi Company.

Gonda, Jan

1976 *Viṣṇuism and Śivaism, A Comparison*. Delhi: Munshiram Manoharlal.

Heiler, von Friedrich

1959 *Die Religionen der Menschheit*. Universal-Bibliothek 8274–8285. Stuttgart: Reclam Verlag.

Hino, Shoun

1981 Pūnashi no ganapatiji ni tsuite (About the Gaṇapati Temple in Poona City) (1). *Tōkai Bukkyō* (*Tōkai Buddhism*) 26: 60–74. Nagoya: Tokai Association of Indian and Buddhist Studies.

1982 Pūnashi no ganapatiji ni tsuite (About the Gaṇapati Temple in Poona City) (2). *Tōkai Bukkyō* (*Tōkai Buddhism*) 27: 89–102.

Hubert, Henri and Marcel Mauss

1964 *Sacrifice: Its Nature and Function*. trans. W. D. Halls. Chicago: The University of Chicago Press.

Ikeda, Kentaro
1979 Pūna no matsuri (Festivals in Poona). *Tōkai Bukkyō* (*Tōkai Buddhism*) 24: 73–89. Nagoya: Tokai Association of Indian and Buddhist Studies.

Johnston, E. H.
1972 *The Buddhacarita* (reprt.). Delhi: Motilal Banarsidass.

Joshi, P. K.
n.d. a *Sārtha Pūjā Saṃgraha.* Poona: Ananta Traders.
n.d. b *Sarva Deva Pūjā.* Poona : Godabole Booksales.

Joshi, Mahadev
1972 *Bhāratīya Saṃskṛtikośa,* Vol. 7. Poona: Bharatiya Saṃskṛtikośa Mandala.

Joshi, S. N. and J. S. Karandikar (ed.)
1940 *Cittapāvana Samājacitra.* Poona: Lakshman Raghunatha Gokhale.

Kane, Pandurang Vaman
1974 *History of Dharmaśāstra,* Vol. 2. Poona: Bhandarkar Oriental Research Institute.

Keith, Arthur Berriedale
1914 *The Veda of the Black Yajus School,* Part 2. Cambridge (MA): Harvard University Press.

Kosambi, D. D.
1962 *Myth, and Reality, Studies in the Formation of Indian Culture.* Bombay.

Limaye, V.M. and V. Bhide
1981 *Puruṣasūkta.* Poona.

Macdonell, A. A.
1965 *Bṛhaddevatā* (reprt.), Part 2. Delhi: Motilal Banarsidass.

Malamoud, C.
1976 Terminer le Sacrifice. *Le Sacrifice dans l'Inde Ancienne.* Paris: Presses Universitaires de France, pp. 155–204.

Manjul, B. T.
1967 *Nityabrahmakarmapaddhati.* Poona: Avinas Prakasan.

Matsubara, Mitsunori
1967 Vishunukyō ni okeru saikōshin sūhai (The Cult of Supreme Deity in Vaishṇavism). *Tōyō Shisō* (*Oriental Thought*) 1: 313–332. Tokyo: Tokyo University Press.

Muir, John
1967 *Original Sanskrit Text* (reprt.), Vol. 1. Amsterdam: Oriental Press.

Oldenberg, Hermann (trans.) [abbr. SBE]
1967 *The Gṛhya-Sūtras Part II.* SBE 30, Motilal Banarsidass, pp. 135-146 (Hiraṇyakeśin)

Renou, L. and J. Fillioza
1947 *L'Inde Classique.* Paris.

Sendye, G.
1981 *Ṛgvedīya Antyeshṭisaṃskāra.* Poona: Joshi Brothers Booksales.

Sirkar, D. C.
1973 *The Śākta Pīṭhas.* Delhi: Motilal Banarsidass.

Sontakke, N. S. and C. G. Kashikar
1946 *Ṛgvedasaṃhitā with the Commentary of Sāyaṇācārya,* Vol. 4. Poona: Tilak Maharashtra Vidyapeeth.

Tachikawa, Musashi
1981 Kamigami to Hindū Kyōto (Dieties and Hindus). *Kami to hotoke no daichi—Indo (The Land of Deities and Buddha—India).* Tokyo: Kōsei Shuppan, pp. 54–87.

Thieme, P.
1939 Indische Wörter und Sitten. *Zeitschrift der Deutschen Morgenländischen Gesellschaft* 93.

Vasudevaśāstri and Paṃṇaśīkara (ed.) [abbr. HBKSam]
n.d. *Hiraṇyakeśibrahmakarmasamuccaya.* Bombay: Nirnaya Sagar Press [in the pothī form].

Wilson, H. H.
1977 *Ṛg-Veda Sanhita.* New Delhi: Cosmo Publications.